INDUSTRIAL MANAGEMENT & ENTREPRENEURSHIP DEVELOPMENT

DR. MUKTA GOYAL DR. EKATA GUPTA

Contents

Foreword

It gives me immense pleasure to announce the launch of a new publication titled "Industrial Management and Entrepreneurship Development "authored by Dr. Mukta Goyal and Dr. Ekata Gupta.

From day one we are made to believe that get a degree, get a good job climb up the corporate ladder just to work for someone else when you have the potential to work for yourself. We spend a fortune on getting an education, getting into debt finally participating in a 9-5 rat race to get a yearly 15 day paid off just to die paying bills. Even if we win this race at end of the day we are still a rat.

Something has to be changed. This book emphasizes change. The change is brought up by something called Entrepreneurship. Dr. Mukta and Dr. Ekata who are having experience as a working professional and also experienced educators share with us the significance of being a good employer than being a good employee, which is guided by their lifelong research and hard work through this exceptional publication. I congratulate both of them for their sheer hard work on this exemplary accomplishment.

Mr. Mukesh Kumar Saxena
Associate Professor
HOD (B.Voc, M.Voc)
Guru Nanak Dev., DSEU
Rohini Campus, New Delhi

Preface

The future of the country belongs to entrepreneurs. The importance of entrepreneurial resource as a critical input in the process of economic development has been widely recognised by the scholars and policy-makers alike. Proper industrial growth can be achieved only through the efforts of the hands of young entrepreneurs. Established companies that fail to adapt to the changes cease to be competition in the marketplace and go out of business. Entrepreneurs are found throughout the world of business because any firm, big or small must have its share of entrepreneurial drive if it is to survive and prosper.

Keeping in view the need of these energetic risk taking learners, we take great pleasure in presenting the book "***Industrial Management and Entrepreneurship Development***". This book is designed with simplicity for students and we are confident that the book will help them.

This book will further help the students to develop as an entrepreneur and reach heights in their career. Any student who reads this book will learn about the entrepreneurial process and its role in economy

Dr.Mukta Goyal
Dr.Ekata Gupta

CHAPTER I

Introduction- Pattern of Economics, Industrial Growth in India

Introduction

Economy

An economy is an institution created by human beings to satisfy people's needs. "An economy is a system where people live," says A.J. Brown. The manner in which he tries to make a living varies from time to time and everywhere. "Getting a livelihood" was easy in ancient times, but it has grown far more complex with the rise of civilisation. It is vital to highlight here that it must be lawful and fair to the person how he or she earns his/her life. Unfair and unlawful methods such as robbery, smuggling can produce revenue for itself but should not be considered as a profit or livelihood system. Therefore, it will be acceptable to term the economy a framework for implementing all economic activity.

System for the Economy

The aim of any economy, with limited or scarce resources accessible and known to a community, is to meet human needs. The production and consumption of products and services can satisfy this need. For production, some economic activities are involved in the elements of production. These financial operations give the economic players revenue which can be spent or saved and invested. Because of these profitable activities and revenues, some nations are growing rapidly, while others are unable to reach such a high development rate. As a consequence, some economies become developed economies, while others stay underdeveloped or underdeveloped.

An economic system is a framework that plans and distributes available services, resources and commodities throughout the country. Economic systems control production aspects that combine wealth, labour, physical resources and people of business. Many businesses, agencies, items, models and procedures are part of an economic system.

Economics Pattern

Economic patterns are generally the whole outcome or consequent outcome of a number of simultaneous economic rules. There are consequently more complicated and multivariate relationships and dependencies in economic patterns than those in economic law.

Economic Patterns

There are economic patterns

1. Capitalist Economy
2. Socialist Economy
3. Mixed Economy

Capitalist Economy

Capitalism is an economic system that owns capital goods by private people or enterprises. The production in the general market – called the market economy rather than the central plan – is a planned economy and command economy. The production of goods and services is based on supply and demand in general markets.

Socialist Economics

The socialist economy, in contrast to a capitalist economic system in which products and services are produced directly for use, produces commodities and services for profit (and therefore indirectly for use). "Socialist production is to be used directly and exclusively.

Mixed Economy

The system that includes characteristics of both capitalism and socialism is a mixed economic system. A mixed economic system preserves private property and enables the use of capital to have a level of economic freedom but also allows governments to engage in economic activity to accomplish social objectives.

Capitalist Economy

The earliest type of economy is the capitalist or free enterprise economy. The policy of "laissez juste," meaning leaving free, was endorsed by past economists. They called for the government's minimal intervention in economic activity. The factors of production are owned by businesses and individuals in a capitalist economy. Entrepreneurship, natural resources, capital goods, and labour are all examples of factors of production. The production of goods and services in a capitalist economy is determined by the general market's supply and demand. Private property, competitive markets, capital accumulation, wage labour, the price system, and voluntary exchange are some of the main characteristics of a capitalist economy. An economy that operates under the premise of a free-market mechanism is referred to be a capitalist economy. It is also known as a system of laissez-faire. The government's role is relatively restricted in a capitalist economy.

Furthermore, in the modern world, there are several types of capitalism, including free-market capitalism, state capitalism, and welfare capitalism. The purest form of capitalism, according to economists, is free-market capitalism. In this type of economic system, private individuals have unrestricted power over what they produce and sell, where they invest, and how much they charge for goods and services. Most modern countries, on the other hand, have a hybrid form of capitalism with some government regulation. Adam Smith's major role in government is to uphold law and order in a country, strengthen national defence, and manage the supply of money. According to Smith, several economic functions are managed by the market system. But government functions in the economy have expanded over a period of time.

The ability of capitalism to provide the best products at the best prices is its primary benefit. In a capitalist economy, there is also an intrinsic reward for innovation. However, there are some drawbacks to this economy. In capitalistic economies, private ownership allows businesses to gain monopoly power in product and labour markets, resulting in significant social injustice.

In a capitalist economy, the government's major tasks are:

a. Develop and uphold the system of the FM

b. Removal of all types of limitation on the operation of FM

c. Increase the efficiency of the FMS through various measures

In Meade's perspective, the government's responsibility in a capitalist economy is as follows:

a. By designing and implementing different fiscal and monetary policies, regulating and managing various economic circumstances, such as inflation and deflation

b. The monopolies and huge companies control their power to evade diverse economic issues such as unemployment and unequal distribution of resources.

c. ownership, by the whole economy, of public services such as trains, education, medical care, water and electricity

d. Prohibition of discrimination and equitable educational and employment opportunities among persons

e. Limiting trade restrictions and union power

f. Preserve law and order, administer justice and protect people's freedoms in an economy

g. The promotion of private enterprises in an economy

h. Establishing a central planning body to contribute to the growth of a broader economy

i. Environmental issues, natural resources extinction and population increase

In pure world capitalism, capitalism is nowadays not perceived in the globe. Capitalist states with their individual governments' active participation in economic growth are known to include the economies of the USA, UK, France, Netherlands, Spain, Portugal, Australia etc.

We may thus infer that the government's primary duty in a capitalist economy is to control and promote the mechanism of the free market. The government should also promote private enterprises to protect the economy's future.

Socialist Economy

In a socialist or centrally planned economy, the government owns and controls all the producing resources in the interests of society as a whole. Decisions are made by a central planning body. A socialist economy is one in which everyone in society owns the same amount of production factors. An economy that is socialist is the polar opposite of a capitalist economy. A democratically elected government is responsible for this type of public or state ownership. Everyone works for wealth in a pure socialist economic system, and wealth is distributed equally among all. Furthermore, a socialist economic system is based on the principle that "what is good for one is good for all."

In a socialist economy, government functions are totally different from government functions in a capitalist one. The government functions as a regulator and a supplementary authority in a capitalist economy. In a socialist economy, on the other hand, the government has a full role to play in practically every economic activity of a nation, such as production, distribution and consumption. The notion of the free-market system is also removed in a socialist economy, not only is the possession of private property allowed to a restricted extent.

Economic and social equality, maximal social protection, communal ownership, economic plan, etc. are characteristic aspects of the socialist economy. Socialist economy's advantages are: no class conflict, no class span, effective resource use, balanced economic development, increased productivity, etc. Socialist economy's demerits include losing consumer sovereignty, planning expenditure etc.

In a socialist economy, private ownership of resources is changed by government ownership. Furthermore, the government centrally plans and supervises all economic activity at the level of the state under the socialist economy. In addition, decisions concerning production, resource allocation, employment, price and consumption restfully on the government or its central planning authority. In a socialist economy, the actions of individuals depend entirely on the government's limits. People are allowed freedom of choice, for example, yet they are subject to the restrictions of the socialist economy's policy framework. Socialism in the world of today the so-called Socialist countries are countries like Russia, China and several countries of Eastern Europe. However, they are changing now, promoting liberalization for their economic progress in their nations.

Mixed Economy

A mixed economy is a type of economy that combines elements of capitalism and socialism. It straddles the line between pure socialism and pure capitalism. Most of the means of production are usually owned and controlled by the private sector, but they are regulated by the government in mixed economic systems. The phrase mixed economy is an economic system that exercises economic management concurrently both public and private. The characteristics of the mixed economy are coexistence between the public and private sectors, individual freedom, the price and pricing mechanism, the motives of profit and social welfare, the cohabitation of the capitalist and socialist elements, etc.

Mixed economies have the advantages of optimal resources allocation, economic and political freedom, quick economic development, minimal concentration of economic strength, etc. The mixed economy demerits include corruption and black marketing, short-lasting characteristics, inefficient operation, poor public sector performance, etc.

The mixed economy describes an economic system, like that of India, aimed to compromise capitalism and socialism. In such an economy the components of government control and market aspects in production and consumption organisation are mixed.

Here the State directly or through its nationalized businesses is doing some production planning, and some are left to private enterprise. This means that alongside each other and complement one another are the socialist sector (i.e., the public sector) and the capitalist sector (i.e. the private sector).

It is a halfway house that may be characterized between a market economy and socialism. Economic control is exerted in a mixed economy, both governmental and private entities. This kind of economy, therefore, seeks to secure both capitalism and socialism's advantages.

A Mixed Economy's Key Characteristics are:

(i)Public and Private Sector Co-existence

The private sector comprises of private-owned industrial entities which function on a profit basis. The public sector comprises of government-owned industrial entities and works on a social basis. In general, each sector's economic activity is divided. In order to control and regulate the private sector, governments utilize their different policies, such as licensing policy, taxes, pricing policy, monetary policy and fiscal policy.

(ii) The Freedom of Individuals.

Economic activity is undertaken by individuals to maximize personal revenues. They may pick and devour any vocation as they choose. But the freedom to abuse customers and workers is not afforded to producers. In the well-being of the people, government places some constraints. For example, government can impose limitations on hazardous items' manufacture and usage. But the privately-held sector has full flexibility for the benefit of society under the rules, regulations and limits established by the government.

(iii) Planning for the Economy

The Government develops long-term strategies and decides on the role of the private and public sectors in economic growth. As such production objectives and plans are created for the public sector, the government is directly under supervision. The private sector is encouraged, encouraged, supported and supported to work according to domestic priorities.

(iv) Mechanism for Prices

In the distribution of resources, prices have an important influence. The policy on managed pricing is applied for specific sectors. Price subsidies are also provided to support the target group by the government.

The government's objective is to enhance mass welfare. For people who are not able to afford to buy the commodities at market rates, the government provides the goods for free or at (subsidised) lower market pricing.

Mixed Contract Merits:

The advantages of the mixed economy are:

1. Economic Freedom- Consumers may behave in accordance with their choices, under a mixed economy. People can pick their occupation completely. People have economic freedom.

2. Monopoly Control - Coexistence between public and private industries in a mixed economy and opportunities for development in the private sector. Monopoly operations are restricted, and numerous laws and regulations have been adopted by the government.

3. Social Welfare - Under this system, government controls the capitalist organizations. The notion of social welfare is the basis of government economic, industrial and financial policy.

4. Resource Planning and Proper Use – Planning is a priority in the mixed economy. All resources are dispersed to various areas of the economy following adequate surveys. This means that resources are used correctly and efficiently.

Thus, individuals have freedom and government assistance to defend the interests of the weaker sectors of the community in a mixed economy at large. The Indian economy is a mixed economy since it contains clearly defined operating and economic planning regions of public and private sectors. Also, mixed economies are now referred to as nations like the US, the UK, etc. that have been regarded as capitalist countries because of their government's active participation in economic growth.

Mixed Economy Demerits:

The demerits of the mixed economy are as follows:

1. Economic System Temporary - As a permanent economic system, mixed economies cannot be sustained. This method was determined to be adequate in the very early stage of development but thereafter its principles declined.

2. **Danger to Democracy** - Socialism can become dominant with the passing of time. The whole economic system would be controlled by the government in such a situation. Thus, democracy might be in jeopardy.

3. **Economic Imbalances** – The mixed economy cannot deliver adequate development as the government tries to preserve the private-public balance. The government's policy is not clear; the outcome is an imbalance in the economy. The finest example of a mixed economy is considered in India. The assessment of an Indian economy is based on ideals enshrined in the Indian Constitution Directive's Principles of State Policy. The principle of democratic governance and democracy requires the state to bring about rapid economic growth in the Indian economy to increase the national and living standards of the masses. According to those Directive principles, it is compulsory for the state to have a democratic form of government.

The Indian Constitution Directive Principles state that the Slate is striving to "advance the well-being of the peoples via the safeguarding and protection of the social order, as effective a way of informing all institutions of national life with justice – social, economic and political."

Within the economic field, the state should guide its policies towards ensuring that ownership and control of the community's material resources are better distributed and that wealth is not concentrated amongst the hands of a few, as well as labour exploitation.

Unless the directive reaches the area of production and distribution, it would be difficult for the state to achieve the purposes suggested. How can the state increase Indian working masses' national income and living conditions unless, with their own involvement, they encourage fast industrialisation? Thus, the State is committed in India to establishing a socialist system in which the current glaring inequalities of wealth are minimised. But the state would therefore not be willing to remove the private company structure, which has done a decent job in the sector of production and distribution despite many blunders and evident handicaps.

Therefore, our mixed economy is the outcome of our dedication to democracy and socialism. As a result, the state sector has grown alongside an expanding private sector.

The Indian economy is a mixed economy, with the co-existence of small, small, medium and big businesses, the private, public, joint, and cooperative sectors. Although a number of areas are overlapping, certain areas will be particularly dedicated to various sectors, or certain industries are excluded from certain regions in order to achieve certain socio-economic objectives.

Difference Between Capitalist Socialist and Mixed Economy

A capitalist economy is an economic system where businesses and individuals own the factors of production while a socialist economy is an economy where each person in society has equal ownership of the factors of production. A mixed economy, on the other hand, is an economic system that has elements of both capitalism and socialism.

Parameters	Capitalist economy	Socialist economy	Mixed economy
Property ownership	Private property	Owner of the public	Public as well as private property
Fixing the price	Prices are influenced by demand and supply market factors.	The central planning authority shall establish prices.	Prices and demand and supply are set by the central planning body.
Production motive	Motive for profit	Social protection	Private sector profit motive and public sector welfare motive
Government's role	No role	Full roles	Full public sector role and minimal private sector role
Competition	Exists	There is no competition	Only in the private sector is available
Revenue distribution	Very different.	Very equal.	Significant disparities

Capitalist, Socialist and Mixed Economies Differences

Therefore, the economic system is a mechanism that plans and allocates country-wide accessible services, resources and goods. Economic systems control production aspects and combine wealth, work, physical resources and employees. Many enterprises, agencies, subjects, models and procedures are included into an economic system. There is no question that the mixed economic system is most appropriate for a large developing country such as India. This is testified to in our experience of growth since independence. If not, India would not have been able to accomplish whatever development and diversity it has achieved had their various responsibilities played by the public, private and other sectors.

Industrial Growth in India

Industrial development has maintained aligned with gross domestic product growth rate in terms of the long-term trend (GDP). During the post-reform period from 1991 to 1992 to 2011-12, the average long-term annual growth of mining, manufacturing and electrical industries was 6.7% compared with GDP growth of 6.9%. Building inclusion in the industry brings this increase to 7.0%. Furthermore, the share of the industry, including building, remained stable in GDP over the period at around 28% (Standard deviation of the average share was very small and this stability was confirmed with a factor of less than 5%) while also staying at 14-16% of the share in manufacture, which is the most dominant in the industry. However, in 2011-12, the manufacturing share of the new series (NAS-2011-12 prices), and the preliminary GDP 2014-15(NS) estimations show that industry's participation in GDP has grown (constant prices) during 2012-13 has risen to around 31-32 percent. The rise in the proportion of the industry, attributable primarily to an increase in the share of production (over 18%), may be related to the new series of methodological improvements, including greater coverage (e.g., the corporate sector), etc. Nevertheless, the aggregate proportion of industrial GDP in China (nearly 40%) and certain East Asian nations remains low compared to (above 30 percent).

India is rapidly becoming one of the world's largest nations. It has numerous lucrative industries, all of which are exponentially increasing. The country does not appear to lose its momentum in the near future either.

Manufacturing has become one of India's fast-growing sectors. India's prime minister, Mr Narendra Modi, has started the Make-in-India campaign to make India a worldwide centre for the Indian economy and the world map. By 2022, the government is aiming at creating 100 million new employees in this industry.

Size of the Market

The gross additional value (GVA), based on the yearly national revenue provided by the Government of Indian, was 5% higher in India at basic current prices from the manufacturing sector over FY16 and FY20 at CAGR. At current prices, the GVA of the industry was projected in FY20PE at US$ 397.14 billion.

Business conditions continue to be good in the Indian manufacturing sector. During FY20, the IIP production component was 129.8. The production of basic metals (10.8%), intermediate (8.8%), food items (2.7%) and tobacco products has experienced significant development in this sector (2.9 percent). The India eight key industries index was 131.9 in FY20. India was 131.9. Indian Industrial Output, assessed by the IIP, grew by 3.6% y-y in October 2020, according to the Ministry of Statistics & Program Implementation.

Investments

With the support of the Make drive in India, India is becoming the hub of high-tech production because global like GE, Siemens, HTC, Toshiba and Boeing have either set up manufacturing plants in India or are in the process of being established, which attracts more than a billion customers on the Indian market and increasing buying power.

India was among the top 10 receivers of foreign direct investment in South Asia in 2019, garnering $49 billion, a 16 percent increase over the previous year according to the United Nations Conference on Trade and Development (UNCTAD).

During the period of April 2000, Cumulative Foreign Direct Investment (FDI) reached US$ 89.40 billion in India's manufacturing sector. By May 2020, the Indian government boosted FDI's automated defence manufacturing from 49% to 74%.

Let's now look at some of the readings to see what they are.

Advanced Manufacturing & Engineering

The campaign "Made in India" is being conducted in India. This was a very effective campaign that brought about a great deal of change in India and the way things are conducted. The Indian government currently focuses on engineering and manufacturing investment and innovation. They are also committed to protecting their intellectual property and constructing the world's largest production infrastructure. Moreover, by concentrating on creating green technology, India has become one of the world's largest automaker manufacturers. The engineering and industrial industries are therefore now flourishing.

The sector of Digital Innovation

More than 500 million internet users are present in India, making it the world's second-largest internet literate population. Yet a few years ago only 19% of Indians had Internet connection, driving the government to build the "Digital India" programme. This effort implies that the digital innovation industry has been fed tones of cash, providing many chances for jobs. It also implies that technology may progress its other areas, such as health care and finance. In the last few years, this industry has so experienced considerable expansion.

Gambling Industry Online

Now that 500 million individuals in India utilize the internet, the online gambling business has now made the way for this. More players desire access to slot machines so they can play or spend their money on sport games. The Indian government has begun legalizing various kinds of internet gambling in order to curb the increase of clandestine play. Offshore operators such as have been permitted to sell their services to Indian clients. The online gaming business in India has gotten stronger and stronger as the popularity of iGaming continues to increase globally in India.

The Energy Sectors

In India, more than 1.35 billion inhabitants are the second biggest population in the world. This indicates that the country has an unbelievably high electricity demand. The energy business has therefore been pushed ahead. Although largely natural gas, crude oil and coal are the basis of the country, the government seeks to concentrate more on renewables. By 2022, it wants its renewable energy industry to have a capacity of 175 GW. As demand for green energy has risen, this has contributed to further propelling India's energy industry.

Industry of Growth

A growing industry is the sector of an economy that, relative to other sectors, has a growth rate higher than normal. Often, new or pioneering sectors that have never been present in the past are growing industries. Their expansion is caused by demand from firms in the area for new goods or services. The technology sector, which produced furious hits with customers and led to billions of dollar estimations for technology businesses in the stock market, is an example of a growing industry.

Comprehension of the Industries of Growth

Several reasons have caused the growth sector to catalyze. One is the emergence of new and creative technologies, which might lead businessmen and startups to build branch-related new goods and services. The reason behind investing in this technology is the promise of exponential future development given the continuously evolving nature of technology.

In the first part of this decade, the smartphone industry, which incorporated several revolutionary technologies into a single phone. Two examples of such a method have been virtual reality (VR) and mechanical study in recent years. VR is a computer-generated, immersive environment capable of simulating a true-life experience. It is applicable in various industries, including VR gaming headsets, driving test simulators and medical school education.

Large data require the processing or identification of patterns and the statistical probability of high volumes of data for the study. Big data companies provide services, such as healthcare, to major companies or industries. The technology has increased start-ups and enterprises in the industry. Investors often evaluate firms on a combination of their present income and future potential for development.

Top Rapidly Increasing Industries in 2020

One of your first thoughts when thinking about starting your own business is: Does my company meet a real demand for the market? Success as a businessman demands answers to the market, and now too many companies are merely remedies for a problem. The Greatest Industries Report of Inc. 2020, a list of the best industries to begin a company, is an indicator for prospective entrepreneurs to search for the best possibilities. We talk to industry specialists each year and collect the latest data to identify economic regions which are prepared for new arrivals. Check out the industries that will welcome the fast-growing start-ups of the future.

The current economic situation has significantly deteriorated. But there's optimism we can get stronger out of it. To do this, we will have to stress the reorganization and improvement of our economy. With this in mind, we are bringing you the leading industries which will witness development in the next years.

Ed-Tech

Online Education

The electronics industry refers to the technologically sophisticated education industry. The Ed tech sector is the responsibility of technology firms operating in the education sphere. It is one of the world's most rapidly developing industries. The Indian market is especially large on the front since the culture has traditionally tended to be educated. Since they founded several firms, such as By Zeus Learning, etc., have done rather successfully.

Digital Commercialisation

Digital Marketing

Digital marketing includes any marketing activities using electronic equipment or the Internet. In India, digital marketing is valued at about 68 billion dollars. Mobile ads have increased to 200 per cent, or $6 billion, via mobile phones or tablets. It is projected that this market would reach $7.8 billion shortly. India also has 110 million mobile internet users, 25 million of them are in rural regions.

Logistics Next Wave

Why it is growing: truckers generate ever more data on driving time, travelled miles and engine performance, which digital cargo brokers may utilise with advanced GPS systems. Furthermore, a 2016 federal legislation compelled several commercial vehicles to report data on their activities electronically. Each person, organisation and product depend on every day on transit, which creates a strong demand. The more technologically-connected transport, the more innovative ideas change from established services to start-ups.

Green Services and Goods

With rising worries over global warming and sustainability, a more environmentally aware populace enters the consumer purchasing market.

Green items in this terrain have gained appeal by delivering superior products with a low environmental effect.

Imperfect Produce, a subscription package for food waste products, has effectively shut down the gap of intention and action by directly addressing its consumers. The firm actively builds stands on farmer's markets and college campuses instead of attempting to attract visitors to their website. This allows customers to obtain information in order to attain their objectives, without having to leave their route.

Endless Technology

'Fintech' is an expression used in the financial industry for technical innovation. Simply put, they relate to firms or services which utilize technology to supply commercial or consumer financial services. In the Indian market, digital payments are becoming truly commonplace, with several firms in the business alone. Fintech's sector can develop to cover many more articles and insurance and training too soon.

Medical and Healthcare

- The CAGR is anticipated to increase global health expenditure by 5% between 2019 and 2023.
- Trends in medical costs in the previous two years have remained stable, but are predicted to grow by 6% by 2020

The present healthcare gaps, particularly high medical and insurance-cost pain spots, provide huge potential for successful startups. Moving away from traditional models and biotechnology specialization, customized health and ageing attention will adapt you to the current demands of the people.

Changes to the healthcare industry blog by big data Hospitals, health equipment, clinical studies, external services, telemedicine, medical tourism, medical insurance and equipment are included in the health care system. It is anticipated that Rs 19,56,920 crore (USD 280 billion) in the Indian health industry would achieve IBEF by 2020. The major drivers to growth include increasing incomes, more knowledge of health, higher prevalence of lifestyle illnesses and improved access to insurance. In India, health insurance is moving forward. Gross direct insured income rose by 17.16% to 32.683.55 crore (USD 4.68 billion) in FY20. In FY20 (up to November 2019).

Gaming

India is now one of the top five mobile gaming countries in the world and will soon be among the top three. The industry should reach 11,900 crores by FY 2022-23 per some forecasts. Around 500 million individuals are playing video games every day in India. While games like these are popular with action-loving youths, those beyond 35 are far more attractive to Rummy and Poker online.

Contribution from Certain Major Companies

India has six major industries traditionally. They include steel and iron, fabrics, jute, sugar, concrete and paper. Moreover, four new industries, petrochemical, automotive, IT and the Indian economy, entered this list. A study of the evolution of these industries can therefore give a clear grasp of the link between their development and

Role of Indian Economic Development Major Industries

The steel and iron industry are some of the major investment sectors. These are usually plants in the public sector. In addition, about 2.5 lakh employees are employed directly by the sector. India is one of the top ten steel manufacturers in the world for the World Steel Association. But we import enormous quantities of steel every year, despite the importance of this business. This is a win-win arrangement since US businesses sell outsourced work to India and China for around 58% of their expenses, and the local economy has worldwide exposure to it.

Banking

In 1969, a decree was issued by the Government of India and 14 major commercial banking banks were nationalized, including 85% of the deposits in the country.

In addition, the banking sector took up the changes in open arms over the years as the technology improved. It has been a new age for the business, from transfers of electronic funds to internet banking.

Sector in India Indian Manufacturing Introduction of Industry Report

Manufacturing has become one of India's fast-growing sectors. India's prime minister, Mr Narendra Modi, has started the Make-in-India campaign to make India a worldwide centre for the Indian economy and the world map. By 2022, the government is aiming at creating 100 million new employments in this industry.

Size of the Market

The gross additional value (GVA), based on the yearly national revenue provided by the Government of Indian, was 5% higher in India at basic current prices from the manufacturing sector over FY16 and FY20 at CAGR. At current prices, the GVA of the industry was projected in FY20PE at US$ 397.14 billion.

Business conditions continue to be good in the Indian manufacturing sector. During FY20, the IIP production component was 129.8. The production of basic metals (10.8%), intermediate (8.8%), food items (2.7%) and tobacco products has experienced significant development in this sector (2.9 per cent). The India eight key industries index was 131.9 in FY20. India was 131.9. Indian Industrial Output, assessed by the IIP, grew by 3.6% y-y in October 2020, according to the Ministry of Statistics & Program Implementation.

Exports of commodities have fallen by 4.78% to 314.31 billion USD in FY20. The manufacturing sector of India improved for the third consecutive month in October 2020, with companies in 13 years in a strong sales increase to the highest degree. MI decreased from 58.9 to a 3-month low of 56.3 in November 2020 in October 2020 which was showing robust manufacturing expansion, in spite of a loss of traction. (Buying Managers' Index)

Investments

With the support of the Make drive in India, India is becoming the hub of high-tech production because global like GE, Siemens, HTC, Toshiba and Boeing have either set up manufacturing plants in India or are in the process of being established, which attracts more than a billion customers on the Indian market and increasing buying power.

India was among the top 10 receivers of foreign direct investment in South Asia in 2019, garnering $49 billion, a 16 per cent increase over the previous year according to the United Nations Conference on Trade and Development (UNCTAD). During the period of April 2000, Cumulative Foreign Direct Investment (FDI) reached US$ 89.40 billion in India's manufacturing sector. By May 2020, the Indian government boosted FDI's automated defence manufacturing from 49% to 74%. In India, investment in the manufacturing sector has become one of the most appealing locations. Some of the most significant investments and advancements in the recent past in this industry are:

Dun & Bradstreet Information Services India signed a Memorandum of Understanding (MoUs) in November 2020 to develop, fund and support an ecosystem for micro, small and medium-sized companies in November 2020. (MSMEs).

The Japan Bank for International Cooperation (JBIC) agreed to offer SBI, (State Bank of India) in October 2020 with USD 1 billion (Rs. 7400 crores) for production and sales financing of Japanese automotive suppliers and dealers and providing car loans to Japanese cars in India.

Tata Group announced intentions to spend Rs. 5,000 crores in Hosur, Tamil Nadu, in October 2020 ($ 673.20 million) to build Apple Component Plant.

October 2020 saw the signing of an MOU with the Tamil Nadu Government to create a state-owned battery and battery management system facilities by Grinntech, a lithium-ion battery and electricity storage system investor-backed start-up.

Five foreign application processes for the manufacture of electronics were authorized by the government of India in October 2020 for the generation of production of Rs. 9 billion (US$ 122 500 billion) for businesses such as Foxconn, Wistron, Pegatron, Samsung, and Rising Star in the following five years.

In October 2020, the Government of India authorized five Indian manufacturing companies, including Micromax, Lava, Padget Electronics, UTL Neolyncs, and Optiemus Electronics, up to Rs. 1.25 trillion ($ 17.02 billion) in phone production over the following five years.

Pegatron, Apple's second-biggest manufacturer, launched its Indian operations after Foxconn in September 2020, with the hiring of legal auditors and the transfer of Rs. 99 lakh (€ 0.1 million) for an initial stock subscription. The action is a prelude to the establishment of an Indian production facility for the Taiwanese electronics manufacturer.

Sterling and Wilson Solar Limited (SWSL) secured in Australia an Rs. 2.600 crore (US$ 368.85 million) engineering procurement building contract (EPC) in May 2020.

Oricon Enterprises engaged in a Joint Venture with Tecnocap Group with its Italy-based office in March 2020, to establish a new lug cap manufacturer firm, Tecnocap Oriental.

Government Initiative

The Indian Government has made a number of efforts to foster a healthy atmosphere for productive growth in the country. In November 2020, 3 lakhs of migrant labourers from 116 districts under Utkarsh, Bihar, Rajasthan, Odisha, Madhya Pradesh, and Jharkhand began skill training in the Ministry for Skills Development and Entrepreneurship. The programme seeks to enhance migrant and rural employees in the after-COVID-19 period by using demand-led skills and orientation to Pradhan Mantri Kaushal Vikas Yojana (PMKVY) 2016-20, a central and central management part (CSCM).

In March 2020, the government authorized the Large-Scale Electronics Manufacturing Producing Incentive Scheme (PLI). The plan provides an incentive to increase local manufacturing and attraction to large-scale investment in the production of mobile phones, including assembly, testing, marking and packaging (ATMP) units.

The government raised FDI in defence-based manufacturing from 49% to 74% in May 2020.

Financial support for the Modified Electronical Manufacture Clusters (EMC2.0) scheme for the development of world-class infrastructure and the provision of shared facilities and equipment through electronic production clusters has been approved by the Union Cabinet in March 2020; (EMCs).

According to the Minister of Statistics and Program Implementation (MOSPI) & Payroll reporting Ministry of Employment in India, in September 2020, there were 10,47, 167 new subscribers* inside the Provident Fund Scheme of Employees.

73 lake persons were trained in the course of 2016-20 under Pradhan Mantri Kaushal Kendra's, whereas 723 were trained by Pradhan Mantri Kaushal Kendras until Jan 2020.

There were around 15,000 ITIs in India from August 2020.

In August 2019, 100 per cent of FDI were allowed by the government in automatic contract manufacturing.

The National Electronics Policy (NPE) enacted in February 2019, envisioned the establishment by 2025 of US$400 billion for the manufacture of electronics in that nation. In the next five years, a global growth rate of 32% was targeted.

The Government wants to expand its contribution of the manufacturing sector in the GDP of India to 25 per cent by 2025 under the Make in India programme.

The Government of India enhanced by two per cent the export incentives offered to MSME sectors in the mid-term review of foreign trade policy (2015-20). The government extended the FTP by one additional year until 31 March 2021 in April 2020.

Road Ahead

India is an attractive location for industrial foreign investment. Several mobile phones, luxury and car manufacturers have established or are seeking to create their production facilities in the nation, among others.

India's production industry might reach 1 trillion US dollars by 2025. by 2025. A single market of US$2,5 trillion in GDP and a population of around

1.32 billion will become a major draw for investors with the introduction of the Goods and Services Tax (GST). India's total laptop and tablet production capacity to reach US$100 billion by 2025 with governmental interventions is expected by the Indian Cellenic Cellular and Electronics Association (ICEA). The government aims at ensuring the holistic growth of the nation through stimulating the development of industrial corridors and intelligent cities. The corridors will help integrate, monitor and build an environment suitable to industrial development, and encourage advanced manufacturing techniques.

Induced Industrialist: Probable's And Obstructions In The Indigenous Community

The industry has established a pattern of elite orientation. A few of the problems that hinder the country's overall industrial development include the concentration of economic power in the hands of few, regional imbalances, industry sickness, loss of the public sector, unsatisfactory relations between workers and workers, insufficient capital and industrial raw materials, changes in the policy of the government and deficient licences. Some of these problems were tried in the following paragraphs. Elite Consumption Model: Another unfavourable element, which only meets the wants of affluent consumers when the output of industrial products is marginally extended. The demands of ordinary people.

Big Houses Growth: The percentage of large households in the private sector's total assets has risen in spite of numerous policy measures implemented by the Government (MRTP Act and the licencing policy. The effect was that economic power was concentrated in a few hands.

Poor Capital Training: Poor capital creation rates are recognised as one of India's greatest constraints for delayed industrial progress.

Political factors: Industrial policies and the British rulers were not at all to the benefit of the country during the pre-Independence period. Thus, over two hundred years of British administration, India remained a primary producer country which eventually delayed the country's industrial revolution.

The elite-based pattern of consumption: Another negative feature is that industrial production only meets the wants of affluent consumers, as well as slightly expanding the demands of ordinary masses.

Growth of Big House: The percentage of large houses in the total assets of the private sector has risen in spite of numerous policy actions implemented by the government (MRTP Act and licensing policy). The effect was that economic power was concentrated in a few hands.

Failure to provide infrastructure: India still falls behind with respect to its infrastructure and is a significant hindrance to the country's industrialization. Thus, in many sections of the nation, in the absence of appropriate transit (trail and road) and communication facilities, industrial growth in these regions could not be achieved, in spite of their considerable development potential.

Agricultural poor performance: Industrial growth in India relies heavily on agricultural sector performance. Another major element in the country's industrial stagnation is the poor performance of the agriculture sector as a result of natural forces.

Gaps between objectives and objectives: The industrial sector could not fulfil its general objectives during the whole planned period save the 1980s. In the first three plans, the current accomplishments were 6%, 7%2, 9%, versus the objective of the 7%, 10.5% and 10.7% industrial growth rate. The gap between the objectives and accomplishments has been widening since the Third Plan.

Using Capacity: a wide range of businesses suffer from capacity under-use. The estimates range from 50 to 60%. According to estimates.

License Policy: The site-approving license policy, capacity, industry type and growth are a typical example of over-state interference and network tapes that are detrimental to industrial development. There have recently been a few cases of political vengeance when the central government has delayed industry authorisation from countries in which the governing party is hostile.

Ministers and leading politicians are presiding over the surrounding businesses to instal industries to grant their permits in their electoral districts. Many of the faults in the licencing policy have been reshuffled with the advent of the liberalisation policy.

Approximately a century later than in industrialised nations, industrialisation started in India. Therefore, it was in India in a childhood stage while the stage was mature in the western countries. Therefore, India has to carry out two tasks: boosting Indus retribalization and equipping itself with the newest electronics, nuclear science and space research technologies. The rate of industrial advancement has slowed down. In addition to becoming victims of 'economics of scarcity' politics, biases and misunderstanding have muddled it.

CHAPTER II

Business Organizations-Silent features of Proprietary,Partnership Private and Public Limited Companies,Cooperative Societies and Public Sector

Introduction

All of the types of a company organization that you need to know. The most important manufacturing and distribution operations take place through the formation of various types of organizations by millions of individuals in different regions of the country.

They are founded on some type of ownership. This option impacts a range of management and financial problems, including the amount of taxes that a contractor should pay, whether the contractor may be sued for outstanding business debts personally or if the firm will automatically die with the death of the contractor.

The firm organization is the most essential option for your company. What your company takes will influence a number of elements that many of them decide on the future of your firm. It is a critical step to align your objectives with your company type, therefore understanding the advantages and disadvantages of each kind is vital.

The organizational forms are

1. Ownership of the Sole(Sole Proprietorship)
2. Company partner
3. Partnership for Limited Liability (LLP)
4. Joint Venture
5. Company of one person (OPC)
6. Private Enterprise
7. Company Public Limited
8. Organizational Company Form
9. Co-op.

Ownership of the sole(Sole Proprietorship)

What is the sole owner's office?

So-called sole ownership may be characterized as a firm or an organization. A single person is a beneficiary of all profit or loss and is solely liable for all risks, is owned, controlled and managed by the individual. It is a common type of company, especially suited for small companies for their first years of activity. This sort of company is generally a service such as hair stalls, beauty shops or small department stores.

Sole ownership definition:

• It is a company kind that is owned, controlled and managed by a single person.

• 'sole' means 'only' and 'owner' notes indicate 'owner.'

• All profits are the only proprietor.

• The only owner shall bear all risks.

• The only owner has completed and unequivocal control.

• Example: beauty salon, barbershop, general store and a single owner's candy business.

Sole proprietorship characteristics:

Training and closure

- The owner himself forms this kind of company organization.
- There is no obligation for legal conventions to start an organization's ownership structure.
- Legal procedures are necessary in some cases or the owner should have a specific company license or certificate. Example: Goldsmith should have a license to manage a medical shop of this kind.
- At his own discretion, the owner can close the business.

Responsibilities

- The solitary owner shall have limitless liability for the sole owner in the single firm.
- In this situation, all obligations are payable to the owner himself.
- He shall thus be accountable for all the debt that can be collected from his personal estates when finances are inadequate, and he shall be liable for any debts that may be recovered from his own estate. Example: A loan from the sweet shop owner is only to pay back the debt to the bank.

Sole carrier of risk and beneficiary

- Only the lone owner bears all of the risks relating to his firm.
- The lone proprietor shall enjoy any earnings or losses made by the firm.

Control

- The sole proprietorship of all rights and obligations, which is why it oversees all business operations.
- Nobody can interfere with the sole proprietor's business activity.
- Only the lone owner can thus change his plans.

No divided entity

- The owner and business are regarded as two different entities under the accounting scheme.
- But the law makes no distinction between the single trader and his business.
- Therefore, the company has no identity with the lone trader, because he is the only person who conducts the business.

Failure to continue business

- Died, imprisoned, physical illness, sole ownership insanity or bankruptcy affects the business directly or may cause the business to shut down. · In the case of the recipient, succeeding or legally sole owner he may manage the enterprise on behalf of the owner.

Advantages of a Sole Proprietorship:

1. Some of the main advantages of a single company are as follows:
2. Speedy making of the decision
3. A lone owner has the right to choose a business.
4. It's simple for a single dealer to make rapid choices since he's the only recipient of all the gains.
5. No need to share any profit, because he's the only investor who invested money in the company.
6. A single proprietor has the power to make his choice on business operations.
7. As a sole proprietor is the sole policymaker of the company, he retains confidentiality of all business-related information.
8. A lone trader thus does not have a legal obligation to bring his accounts to the public view.

Direct stimulus

- The one owner is the only one who receives all of the benefits that the business offers.
- Therefore, the solitary owner's profit is motivated to make a further effort for greater advantage and growth in the firm. The one owner is the only owner.

Realization sense

- A small company's success creates the impression that the business has achieved its aims and motivates it.
- There is therefore a sense of personal satisfaction from obtaining profit or long-term advantages.

Sole Proprietorship Constraints:
Some of the major limitations of a single owner include:
(1) Resources limited

- A lone proprietor's resources are restricted to his parents' savings and loans.
- The banks also hesitate or refuse to give the lending of long-term loans or extend the length of long-term lending because of the financial situation poor for the enterprise.
- The reasons above are why the business is usually tiny.

(2) Firm life

- The owner and his company are the same thing and the life of the business is limited owing to the lack of a successor or an heir.

(3) Unlimited liability

- If the single owner fails to pay the bills, the creditors would not only be liable for their commercial property, but also for their personal property because of the business' collapse.
- It's too hazardous to take a huge loan and it's also putting the pressure on the lone business owner.

- Therefore, this is why the traders alone will not take a risk to the company's existence and growth.

(4) Management capacity limited

- All obligations to perform the business must be accepted by the only owner.
- Sometimes the householder needs to handle all management tasks, such as sales, purchases, marketing, sales, business with customers, etc.

Public and Private Limited Enterprises Partnership

What does a partnership mean?

A partnership is a sort of business in which two or more persons form and manage a company jointly. The three major forms of corporations are common partnerships (GP), limited partner companies (LPs) and partnerships with limited liability (LLP).

One of the greatest perks is that the company is a flux company. Any revenue earned in a partnership will thus be considered as the partners' personal income. This implies that it gets taxed just once. In contrast, a company's owners incur double taxation. This is because the revenue of the company is once taxed and the personal income of the owner is then taxed twice.

One of several forms of business is partnerships. Single ownerships, limited liability companies (LLC) and corporations also form part of other kinds of enterprises.

Characteristics of the Corporate partnership Firm

The different features of the type of partnership of a commercial organization may be summarized as follows, based on the definition of partnership as above:

(a) Two or more people: two persons at least are necessary to create a partnership. For banks, the upper limit is 10 people, and for other companies 20. The partnership becomes illegal if the number surpasses the aforementioned limit and the ties between the partners cannot be termed partnership.

b) Contractual relationship: a partnership between individuals that have decided to join hands should be established by an agreement. Such individuals should be contractually competent. Minors, crazy people and bankrupt people are not thus eligible for partnership. A minor, however, may be allowed to benefit the company, i.e., without losing obligations, he may partake in the profits.

(c) Earnings and Business Sharing: Partners must have to agree on the sharing of the company's profits and losses. When two or more individuals share the revenue of common property, it is not a partnership.

(d) Lawful business existence: the company from which the individual has committed to share the profit must be legal. Any arrangement that allows smuggling, illicit marketing, etc. cannot in the eyes of the law be termed partnership.

(d) Connection of Principal Agent: The partners must have an agency relationship. Both the principal and the agent of the company are partners. When a partner deals with other parties it functions as the agent of other partners, while also becoming the principal for the other partners.

(e) Limitless responsibilities: unlimited responsibility exists for the partners of the company. Both together and individually, they are responsible for the company's debts and responsibilities. If the company's assets are inadequate to fulfil the liabilities of the company, the partners' personal possessions may also be used for this reason. However, a small partner's liability is restricted to the number of his profit shares.

(f) Voluntary registration: The partner company's registration is not obligatory. However, an unregistered company has some restrictions which make it almost obligatory to register. The restrictions of an unregistered company are as follows:

- The company may not use external parties, even though external parties may prosecute them.
- In cases of conflict between the partners, a dispute cannot be settled by a court of law; The Company cannot demand any adjustments to or from any third party for any sum due.

Partner Types

In these business structures, there are two main categories of partners: general partners and limited partners.

Partner general: a partner in charge of management. They are in charge of the company operations. General partners are, in addition, completely responsible for company debts, as well as facing limitless responsibility. That implies they can take their own assets to satisfy liabilities or legal proceedings.

Limited partner: a partner having a financial investment, but no responsibility for management. As such, limited partners are not actively managed, they cannot be held personally responsible for the debts of the firm. The one partner that might lose most is his investment in the enterprise. Limited partners are essentially the most similar to corporate shareholders.

Partnership Types

Three basic kinds of partnerships exist, as indicated. The pros and cons of each variety are their own.

Partnership General (GP)

The simplest fundamental kind of partnership is general partnerships (GP). It is the easiest to build and the cheapest to keep. They are simpler than businesses and even other partnerships. When partners start commercial operations, a general partnership is created immediately. No official documentation is necessary. In a GP there are just general partners.

Fortunately, in the event of bankruptcy or death, there are measures to prevent dissolution. This sort of company arrangement is generally followed by a partnership agreement. Partners may add provisions stating that following the death of a partner the business will continue and providing for a method through which the interests of the dead will be shared among the other partners.

Partnership Limited

Limited partnerships (LPs), which give more protection to partners, are a kind of partnership. In an LP, at least one general partner is responsible for managing business and assuming unrestricted liability. The other partners are limited partners who have financial interests in the company and do not bear personal responsibility for the enterprise.

Limited partners share the firm's earnings, but they can only lose as much as they put in the company.

Partnership for Limited Liability

The expansion of the GP is limited liability partnerships (LLP). An LLP is basically a GP in which all partners are shielded from other partners' activities. Basically, there is minimal responsibility for all partners. This is distinct from an LP where at least one unlimited liability partner must be present.

LLPs keep their status as tax transfers, making them very comparable to limited liability corporations (LLC).

Although LLPs may seem attractive in comparison to GPs and LPs, many jurisdictions limit them to particular occupations. These include attorneys, physicians and accountants. A company owner cannot thus always form an

LLP.

Agreement on Partnership

The partnership agreement is a key component of this sort of business. The Agreement describes how the company operates in terms of conflict resolution or profit allocation. This is one of the company's most essential papers and may prevent many possible negative effects. As noted above, for instance, the agreement should define how the interest of a partner in the firm is transmitted after death. This would allow a GP to remain in place even when one of the partners is gone. In addition, the agreement should record and describe the ratio of ownership between the partners' financial contributions.

Private and Public Limited Companies

Private enterprises are held privately—no surprise here. In most situations, this means that the firm belongs to its founders, management or private investors.

A public enterprise, on the other hand, is a business that, by means of an initial public offering (IPO), has sold all or some of itself to the public. That means that the shareholders have a right to some part of the assets and earnings. A public limited company is a listed corporation and stocks are traded publicly. A public limited company A private limited business, on the other hand, is not traded on the stock exchange. Only its members hold it secretly.

What is a private Limited Company?

The most basic and common form of business registration in India is a Private Limited Company. It is possible to register with at least 2 persons. Limited protection of owners' responsibility, capacity to grow shareholdings, distinct status as the legal entity makes it the most preferred company structure for millions of family-owned and professionally managed small and medium enterprises.

A private limited enterprise is a private owner-owned enterprise. Such a company confines the responsibility of the owners to their shareholders and bans stockholders from participating in the public sector.

Minimum Private Limited Company Requirement:

• a Minimum number of two adult managers.

• An Indian Citizen and an Indian Resident must be one of the directors of a private limited corporation.

• Foreign national may be the other director(s).

• Two shareholders of a corporation should also be necessary.

• The stockholders may be real or artificial entities.

Private Limited Company benefits:

There are several benefits for a private limited company here.

In private limited companies, there is a limited danger of personal assets.

Pvt. Ltd. Co. is an independent legal entity.

There would be a limited liability for members in the Private Limited Company.

A company's shares restricted by shares can be transferred to any other person by an equity shareholder. The transfer is easy when compared to the transfer of an interest in an enterprise operating in the form of a private enterprise or partnership.

Just as a person may bring proceedings against another person on his or her own behalf, an enterprise that is an independent legal entity may take a suit and prosecute in his or her own name.

An enterprise has 'perpetual succession that lasts or remains continuous until terminated lawfully.

The previous minimum share capital number for a private enterprise was Rs. 1,00,000, however, the minimum capital obligation is now absent. Consequently, there are no fund needs under pressure.

It is possible to receive finance through the transfer of shares in a private limited business.

Private Company Drawbacks:

• One of the major disadvantages for a privately held limited company is that it restricts the ability of its articles to transfer its shares.

• In any event, the number of members cannot exceed 200 in a private limited corporation.

• The privatized limited business also has a disadvantage since it cannot release a public prospectus.

The registration of an equity-limited private corporation takes longer duration and entails a process and expense not applicable to single ownership and company names. Once a private limited company has been registered, however, it has several powers and privileges. If your company runs into problems, it will shield your personal assets with what is called a corporate veil, with the company and not the directors still responsible for any debts, losses or legal claims. Shareholders must not be obliged to pay more than the value of the shares they took in the enterprise.

What is a Public Company?

Public companies are firms trading in public exchange stocks. public companies are companies. Through the acquisition of shares of the firm, investors can become shareholders in a public corporation. The firm is classified as a public corporation since any interested investor can buy publicly owned shares of the Company.

A public business is a firm with a public initial public bid authority for the issuance of registered securities (IPO) and listed on at least one stock exchange. A public enterprise is not authorized simply after a certificate of incorporation is granted to commence its business activities. In order to be eligible for public service, a trade certificate needs be obtained.

An annual general meeting (AGM) should be held by a public business where the shareholder's vote to elect new board members, discuss policy and create new policies, goals, and regulations which guide the firm's activities. The shareholders are entitled to a share of the company's earnings and the profits are split by the number of shares owned by each shareholder.

A large number of public firms began out as private companies and became publicly available to support their projects through a broader pool of money financing their company projects or activities. A first public offering is part of the process of establishing a public business (IPO). The IPO should be approved and comply with all regulatory requirements by the Securities and Exchange Commission (SEC). The aim of the IPO is to generate funding by selling stock to the public for the issuing business.

The Public Limited Company's Advantages are as follows:

1. **Members:** A corporation needs to have at least 7 members in order to be public (maximum unlimited).
2. **Steady Firm Growth:** Private Limited Companies can adopt technology to develop quickly their business by providing enough financial accessibility.
3. **Capital increase through issuing equities:** capital insufficiency is unavoidable during a business however, unlike the private limited company, the public limited company has a possibility to raise equity through the public share issuance.
4. **Funds may be moved quickly:** PLC shares can simply be transferred. As the public limited company's equities are traded on bourses, more prospective shareholders are driven.
5. **Access to extra financing:** Banks and financial organizations often provide loans at advantageous rates to Public Limited Companies. In

addition, PLC has the right to negotiate loan reimbursement terms and circumstances.

6. **Liability restricted:** public business responsibility is limited. liability limited. No shareholder shall be liable for payment on an individual basis. The public limited corporation is a separate legal entity, which includes every shareholder.

The Public Limited Company's disadvantages are:

Prospectus: The issuance of prospectuses is compulsory for a public undertaking since the public is encouraged to subscribe to its shares.

Higher paid-up equity: In contrast to a private limited enterprise, public limited company training costs are significantly higher (INR 5 Lakh) (INR 1 Lakh).

More stringent rules: A PLC is required to adhere to a number of laws. These legislative standards are intended to protect the shareholders' interest in the Company.

Transparent transactions are necessary: since companies offer publicly their shares, they must provide comprehensive information on their prospective development and commercial activities. • Transparent dealings are essential. There is no privacy and nothing PLC can conceal; even media coverage is provided to their account data.

Loss of management control: once a private business becomes public, it becomes more difficult to manage the business. The firm owner cannot decide unilaterally any more.

Difference between private enterprise and private enterprise?

An artificial person formed by law is an enterprise at its core. This is a partnership of persons with a separate legal existence, a constant succession and a joint identity. The capital, subject to certain restrictions, must normally be split into transferable shares.

The most prevalent forms are private (Pvt. ltd.) and public enterprises (ltd.). It has its own advantages and disadvantages both for private and public limited enterprises.

A contractor must select the kind based on his financial schemes. Consider both private and public ltd firms' important aspects.

The table below will help us understand better the distinctions between the two:

Feature	PVT. Company	Public Limited Company
Minimum Members	There should be at least 2 members.	There should be at least 7 members.
Maximum Members	There can be a maximum of 50 members.	There is no limit so as to the number of members.
Minimum Directors	There should be minimum 2 Directors.	There should be minimum 3 Directors.
Suffix	Pvt. Ltd.	Ltd.
Statutory Meeting	Voluntary	Mandatory
Public Subscription	Not Allowed	Allowed
Share Transferability	Restricted. Not freely transferable.	Freely Transferable.
Quorum Requirements	2 members personally present.	5 members present personally.
Commencement of Business Operations	On receipt of Certificate of Incorporation.	On Receipt of Certificate of Commencement of Business.
Minimum Paid Up Capital	Rs. 1,00,000/-	Rs. 5,00,000/-

Difference between Private Company and Public Limited Company

The foregoing elements showed us the differences between the two companies. In general, the legal requirements of a private company are less than those of a public company. Publicly owned and traded, a public undertaking is compatible with a private undertaking since private undertakings are private.

There are clear and unequivocal benefits to the public registration of limited companies. But PLCs must also take the disadvantages into consideration. Finally, it reduces to stability and risks whether or not you opt to form a limited public enterprise. You can benefit from the benefits of the asset management company by providing significant improvements and new opportunities for development if you feel your companies are established and have the financial support, growth potential, legal expertise and guidance to bring people into asset ownership.

Cooperative Society

A cooperative kind of company is different from other forms of enterprise. It is a voluntary group of individuals with jointly held funds, organized on the democratic concept of equality, who work together to provide services and profit for their needs via mutual action.

The main purpose of building a cooperative is to prevent the weaker economic sectors of society from being oppressed by the more organized economic part of society. There is no new notion in a cooperative society. This is practically a universal notion in all countries. The cooperative society is active in every country and is represented by agriculture, food, banking, healthcare etc. In all areas.

The cooperative society is created to defend the interests of the weaker parts. It is a freelance association of people who are motivated by members' well-being.

Cooperative Society characteristics

The membership is also voluntary as it is a voluntary organization. An individual is free to enter a cooperative community and can leave whenever he wishes. Membership is available to anyone regardless of religion, sex and caste.

Registration is required for a cooperative company. The cooperative society is an independent juridical personality in the society.

The admission or leave of its members should not influence it. The members of the cooperative company have limited liability. The amount paid by the members as capital is restricted to the extent of the liability.

The elected board of management is empowered to decide. Members shall have the right to vote by electing the members of the management committee.

The cooperative society is based on the idea of mutual assistance and well-being. Therefore, it is dominated by the principal of the service. If there is a surplus, it will be divided up among the members in accordance with the company regulations.

Advantages:

1. Easy Training: The establishment of a cooperative society is easy compared to the foundation of a corporation. Ten adults can create an organization voluntarily and register it with the Co-operative Registrar. The establishment of a cooperative organization does not also entail costly and extensive legal processes.

2. Tax Advance: a cooperating company is free from income tax and surcharge on its revenue to a limited extent, unlike the other three types of corporate ownership. In addition, the stamp and registration cost will also be excluded.

3. Everlasting Existence: There is a separate legal entity in a cooperative company. Therefore, the death, insolvency, retirement, love, etc. of members of a cooperative organization do not influence their lifetime.

4. Restricted liability: Like the structure of the firm ownership, the responsibility of members in the cooperative societies is limited to the amount of their capital.

5. Democratic administration: management of the cooperative society, regardless of the number of shares owned by it, is committed to the management board lawfully chosen by the members on the basis of a 'one member one - vote.' In cooperative societies, the proxy is not authorized. Cooperative administration is therefore democratic.

6. Social service: self-help and mutual assistance is the fundamental concept of co-operatives. Co-operatives thus nurture their fellow members' sense and instill in them moral principles to make them live better.

7. State Assistance: Government co-operatives have been embraced as an efficient socio-economic transformation instrument. The Government thus gives cooperative societies a range of grants, loans and financial support, in order to improve their operations.

8. Open Membership: Co-operative partnerships are open to everybody regardless of caste, colour, creed and economic position. The maximum members are not limited.

Disadvantages

The cooperative, while its many advantages, nevertheless has certain disadvantages which must be taken into consideration thoroughly before choosing this way of owning a firm.

The Main Drawbacks are as Follows:

1. Corruption: Lack of profit motives in a sense leads to managerial fraud and corruption. That is evident in the officials' own misuse of cash.

2. Lack of Mutual Interest:a cooperative society's success depends on the greatest trust amongst its members. However, not all members have a cooperative spirit. Lack of such a spirit creates reciprocal rivalry amongst the members.

3. Lack of Interest: compensated co-operative company office-bearers are not concerned about the operation of societies because of lack of an incentive for profit. The success of business demands continuous work in a period of time that in many cooperatives does not exist. The cooperatives are thus dormant and stopped.

4. Lack of secrecy: A cooperating company should report to the Registrar of Cooperative Societies on their yearly finances and reports. It is therefore quite difficult for her to keep her business secret.

5. Business lack Acumen: Cooperative partnership members usually lack business acumen. If these people become board members, societal affairs are not anticipated to be carried out properly.

Public Sector

Public sector sectors include public services and government services such as military, law enforcement and infrastructure, public transit, public education, health care and public services, including public service officials and those working in government, bridges, tunnels, supplies of water, sewers, electric grids, telecommunications, etc. The public sector might offer services that cannot be omitted by a non-payer (e.g., street lighting), which benefit society as a whole and not only those who use the service. State or public undertakings are self-financing commercial undertakings under public control that sales and typically function on a commercial basis and supply different private products and services.

Public sector organizations are a member of either the private or voluntary sector. The private sector is made up of the economic sectors whereby the owners of the company are meant to profit. A variety of non-profit organizations that emphasize civilian society are involved in the voluntary, civil and social sectors.

Public Sector Characteristics

State ownership: The State must be given ownership of the company. It may be in the character of ownership by central, state or municipal governments, or it may also be inherent in any instrumentality by the state.

State control: the government's administration and operation is governed by the public enterprise. The Government has a direct duty to manage the business through different methods and to control it through a range of agencies and procedures.

Public Responsibility: Public companies owe public financing accountability to citizens. The parliament and its committees, ministries, audit institutions and other specialized organization's are responsible for this.

Autonomy: under some conditions, public enterprises operate with the most autonomy. They are free to meddle with their management and business from day today.

Coverage: All regions and activities are covered by the public enterprise. The sphere of activity is scarcely covered by public business operations.

Role Of Public Sector And Private Sector Economics

Introduction

In order to achieve country economic progress, the public sector and the private sector play a major role. An impact of their role on socio-economic growth is seen in the country. In 1961, the first five-year plan was launched in a powerful and leading Bhutanese public sector. In addition, the Bhutanese economy was driven by its development. In a growing country like India, the public sector has been well placed to achieve methodical and planned development. The private sector is unable to make the necessary effort to expand its numerous sectors concurrently in a nation like India which has multi-dimensional challenges.

During the sixth FYP, privatization was proclaimed to play an even more significant role for the private sector in supporting economic growth and as a source of jobs. Since then, the private sector has been strengthening socio-economic growth with the Royal Government of Bhutan, and Bhutan has been regarded as one of Southeast Asia's fastest developing countries. But in terms of financial, human resources, efficiency and management, both industries are still underdeveloped. In addition, the development of both the public and private sectors has various obstacles. Therefore, the public sector gives the minimal essential impetus to lead the economy towards self-sustained growth in order to provide the necessary support for the country's development goal. It is now widely known that in the earliest stages of its growth, public service plays a beneficial role in the country's economic development by establishing the basis for a solid industrial structure.

Private and Public Sector Definition

The private sector is defined as the segment of the economy in which an individual or a group of individuals owns the production elements, with maximization of profit as the main aim.

Only for the sake of profit and its consumer rivals are private products created by the private sector. Only one individual who pays has no social advantage, and so is exclusive in nature, enjoys benefits. Private entrepreneurs are not societal welfare but self-benefit. Competition is the only thing between every private contractor, which leads to effective utilization of resources. The public sector refers to the component of the national economy owned by the whole society and operated for social well-being, according to Wilson & Clark. There is many kinds of governance in the public sector (central, state and local). It offers fundamental products or services that the private sector, for example, schools, roads, etc. neither can nor can supply.

Here are some of the significant relative public sector functions in a country like India's economic development:

(a) Promoting rapid economic development by filling industrial structure gaps;

(b) Promoting adequate economic growth infrastructure;

(c) undertaking economic activity in strategically important fields of development in which the private industry may distort the mindset of national objectives;

(d) Monopoly monitoring and power concentration;

e) To create and improve sufficient employment opportunities in various sectors through heavy investments;

(f) to achieve self-reliance, as required, in various technology;

(g)to eliminate reliance on external aid and technology;

(h) to exert social control and regulation in various government financial institutions;

The relative role of the Indian private sector: India, as a mixed economy, plays a major role in achieving rapid economic development for India's private sector. In the fields of industry, trade and services, the Government has established a specific role to the private sector.

Private sector contributions are shown below:

1. Helpful for development: The private sector is a significant part of economic development according to Schumpeter Peter. It improves the industrialization process. All private contractors labor for the sake of profit. In fact, the new commodities, new manufacturing processes, new plant equipment and machinery have been a major factor in introducing them.

2. Generation of jobs: In the country, the private sector has a major role in creating jobs. A considerable number of cottage units are under private sector ownership, small and big size. In comparison to major companies, this shows that small-scale and cottage industries create four times as many jobs. For employment, the private sector share was 51,2 percent compared to 44,3 percent for the public sector, according to figures from 2001-02

3. Most Important Sector: In the Indian economy, the importance of the private sector is great despite the huge progress of the public sector throughout the plan era. The number of private sector businesses in the

2001–02 period was 1, 10, 634, compared to the total number of firms of 1,28,549, based on the attested figures for the industrial growth of the nation. Otherwise, only 11,67o undertakings in the public sectors were under private sector management cf 86.1% of the total firms.

4. Industry contribution: According to the Resolution of 1956, "the private sector is able to establish businesses that produce intermediate products and machinery." Many ultra-modern industries under private sector management are built. It comprises numerous beneficial industries for consumers, such as sugar, petroleum, textile, paper, spice, and fast-food or semi-finished industries.

5. Agriculture contribution: India is an agribusiness. Agriculture is over 22 percent, as are activities linked to it such as fisheries, poultry, cattle raising, livestock breeding, dairy production, etc. On the other hand, approximately 60% of the workforce in this field is employed. Therefore, the private sector controls this huge agricultural industry.

Even the private sector has a prominent role to play in their growth in the fields of capital goods, iron and steel engineering, chemical, engine etc. The operations of few private industries in the post-liberalization phase (after the New Industrial Policy was introduced in 1991). Table 3 displays net sales in India in 2004 of the 10 largest private sector giants.

6. High potential: Most of the small-scale and cottage businesses use interspine labor technology and provide significant job prospects. The private sector belongs to these industries. Some 80% of the total number of employees is engaged in private entities, organized or disorganized. Approximately three-fourths of national revenue contributes to the private sector. In addition, this sector also plays a key role in increasing the economy's gross domestic savings (CDS) and the development of domestic gross capital (GDCF).

In the growth and expansion of this set of industries, the private sector plays a beneficial role. Furthermore, the private sector is also responsible for developing small-scale and cottage enterprises.

Finally, in the growth of the country's tertiary sector, the private sector also has its part. The private sector manages the whole services sector, which provides the people in general with numerous sorts of services. The private sector also manages the complete wholesale and retail commerce in the country quite rationally. In addition, the main component of transport is also controlled by the private sector, in particular in road transport. As the Indian economy has been further liberalized in recent years, the private sector is allocated considerably more responsibility in different areas of economic activity.

Non-rival in consumption public goods which may be derived by any person via consumption. No one may object, for example, to using the road, and the right to consume is equal. However, the amount of enjoyment that comes from one person to the other. The private and social-welfare activities in the public sector are non-financial.

The public sector does not carry out operations for the exclusive advantage of society as a whole.

Monopoly

What is Monopoly?

'Monopoly' definition

A single-seller market structure that sells a unique product on the market. The vendor is unable to compete in a monopolistic market, as it is the only seller without near substitutes. A monopoly is defined by the dominance of a firm and its products in a sector or industry. Monopolies can be viewed as an extreme outcome of free markets since, without any limitation or restriction, one business or group is sufficiently large to possess all or almost all of the markets of a specific product or service (goods, supplies, commodities, infrastructure and assets). The word monopoly is commonly used to characterise an enterprise which controls a market completely or almost entirely.

One single market provider is a complete monopoly. Monopoly power exists, for the purposes of regulation, if a single company controls 25% or more of a given market. In vertical integration certain firms become monopolies. The whole supply chain is controlled from manufacture to commerce. Others are adopting horizontal integration. You purchase competitors until they're the only ones remaining. 1

Some people have government rules that provide them a market, like utilities. Governments are doing so, since they do not accept the interruptions that may result from free-market forces, to assure power production and distribution. Monopolies are created For a number of reasons, monopolies can emerge, including:

Formation of monopolies

Monopolies can form for a variety of reasons, including the following:

If the company has a rare resource exclusively, such as Microsoft which has a windows brand, it is the sole company that may exploit that resource.

Governments may award Oliver Cromwell a firm Monopoly status, for example, the Post Office, in 1654. In 2006, as the market opened for competition, the Royal Mail Group ultimately lost its monopoly position.

The manufacturer may hold patents for designs or copyright for ideas, characters, photographs, sounds or names that provide it exclusive rights to sell a service, such as a monopoly on its own materials by an artist songwriter.

After the merging of two or more businesses, a monopoly could be established. As this reduces competitiveness, such fusions are closely regulated and can be avoided when the two companies attain a combined market share of 25 percent or more.

Although monopolies may be different among industries, they tend to share common features, including:

Higher entry barriers: Competitors can't access the market and monopolies may simply block competition by acquiring competitors from building its footing in an industry.

Single seller: just one seller is on the market, which means the firm will be identical to its industry.

Price maker: the monopolistic company determines whether to offer the goods, and maintain its pricing in check without competition. Monopolies can therefore increase prices at will.

Scale savings: Monopolies can typically yield less than smaller firms at lower cost. Monopolies can acquire enormous inventory quantities, such as a discount on volume. A monopoly can therefore so cut its prices that lesser rivals cannot exist.

The monopolist can obtain super-normal gains, region PABC, without near replacements.

The most monopolistic power may be derived from a monopolist without a replacement.

Key Indicators

High barriers to entry: Competitors cannot enter the market, and the monopoly may easily restrict competition by gaining competition from expanding its footing in an industry.

Single seller: just one seller is available on the market, which means that the firm has the same functioning as the industry.

Price maker: The monopolistic company determines the price of the product which it sells and its prices are checked without competition. Monopolies can therefore increase prices at will.

Scale savings: A monopoly might typically generate less than smaller businesses. Monopolies can acquire enormous inventory quantities, such as a discount on volume. A monopoly can therefore so greatly cut its prices that lesser rivals cannot survive. Essentially, because of the scope of their production and distribution networks such as storage and shipping, monopolies may wage price wars at less cost than any rival in the indigenous market.

Monopoly Types: **Simple monopoly:** A simple monopoly company charges a consistent price to all purchasers for its output. While a discriminating monopolistic company charges various purchasers varying rates for the same goods. In a single market a simple monopoly is operating in more than one market, a discriminating monopoly.

Pure monopoly and imperfect monopoly: pure monopoly is the monopoly type in which the supplies of a product that has no replacement, not even a distant, are controlled by a single company. It has an absolute power of monopoly. It is exceedingly unusual to have such a monopoly. Imperfect monopoly, however, indicates limited monopoly. It refers to one company that provides a product which has no near replacements. The level of monopoly in this situation is less than ideal and it concerns the proximity of an alternative to be available. In actuality, such imperfect monopolies occur numerous times.

Natural monopoly: If natural reasons establish a monopoly, the monopoly is termed a natural monopoly. In mica production now, India has monopoly while in nickel production, Canada has monopoly. These monopolies have brought these countries into existence.

Legal monopoly: if an individual is monopolized by law in the country or obtains it.

Industrial monopolies or Public Monopolies: in the common interest of the country if some industries within the public sector are nationalized by a government that creates industrial or public monopolies. For instance, the Industrial Policy Resolution 1956 in India explicitly sets out the Central Government's sole monopoly in specific areas such as weapons, ammunition, nuclear power, rail and air transport. This creates industrial monopolies through legislation.

Key Takeaways

- A monopoly refers to the dominance of one area or industry by a business and its product offerings.

• Monopolies are viewed as the ultimate outcome of free capitalism and are frequently used to characterize an entity with absolute or almost total market dominance.

• When significant entry barriers are present, natural monopolies may exist; the Company has a patent on its products, or governments are permitted to offer vital services.

Price Restriction

What Are Price Restrictions and How Do They Work?

The legal minimum or maximum prices set for particular items are referred to as "price restrictions." In a free market, price restrictions are usually imposed by the government. They are typically used as a direct economic intervention to restriction the affordability of particular products and services, such as rent, gasoline, and food. While price restrictions may make certain goods and services cheaper, they can also cause market disruptions, producer losses, and a perceptible change in quality.

Important Takeaways

Price restrictions are minimum or maximum prices set by the government for specified commodities and services.

To manage the affordability of goods and services on the market, price restrictions are implemented.

Price floors refer to the lowest prices, while price ceilings refer to the highest prices.

These restrictions are only effective for a very limited period of time.

Price restrictions can lead to issues including shortages, rationing, poor product quality, and illegal markets in the long run.

Price Restrictions: An Overview

Price restrictions, as previously stated, are a type of government-mandated economic intervention. They're intended to make items more inexpensive for consumers, but they're also frequently employed to help drive the economy in a particular way. These limits may, for example, be deemed necessary in order to reduce inflation. 1 Prices set by market forces, which are determined by producers due to supply and demand, are the polar opposite of price regulations.

CHAPTER III

Entrepreneurship- Entrepreneurial qualities, Selection of product,Estimation of Expenditure Resources of Capital Financial Agencies

Introduction

To be business might imply to know your industry inside and to use this knowledge to generate new chances. Being business may be an open exchange of ideas and celebrate so-called failures as learning and experiences.

Nobody has been born as an entrepreneur, and everybody is a prospective candidate for entrepreneurship. In other words, the personality of a contractor is generally seen as an important part of its success or failure.

So, think about your actual motive and the potential to succeed before you take the jump. A business needs many other talents, so you know who you are best. Start or take over a business.

Hard-working professionals have many features in common, therefore the attributes of a successful entrepreneur don't seem surprisingly comparable. Successful businessmen have inherent inventiveness and an effort to excellence. They are enthusiastic and confident. They are self-running, disciplined and receptive to new ideas.

10 Entreprenuer Qualities

1. Controlled

Successful business people concentrate on working. They remove all obstacles and diversions and describe strategies to achieve them. Without neglecting their long-term objectives, they focus on their company's daily activities. Successful entrepreneurs are sufficiently disciplined to take every day steps toward their goals.

2. Trust

Businesses don't wonder if they can succeed or if they're deserving of success. You are certain that you will make your company successful. They radiate that trust in whatever they do.

3. Open-Minded

Contractors know that every incident and scenario is a chance for business. Ideas on processes and efficiency, skills for individuals and possible new companies are continuously being produced. They always seek innovative methods to improve the existing systems and procedures. Enterprises are unable to imagine a product that solves an issue, while it might not appear conceivable at the moment. You are capable of looking at and focusing everything around you on your goals.

4. Self-starter

An entrepreneur is distinguished by many characteristics. Self-starter persons tend to be more successful due to their inherent capacity for time and performance management. Entrepreneurs realize that they should start themselves if anything has to be done. They set the criteria and ensure that the initiatives go in that direction. They are proactive, not waiting for approval from anybody. They are looking for solutions, like Inc and Go, to decrease the difficulties of workplace start-up and other operations.

5. Concrete

Many businesses are founded because an entrepreneur feels they can perform better work than someone else. You have to win in the sports you play and must win in the companies you build. Enterprises will promote the success record of their own firm. In order achieve excellence in business, entrepreneurs are able to investigate all their possibilities and to pursue their goals aggressively. They are ready to face whatever obstacles they might face so they can surpass them.

6. Creatorship

A great contractor is innovative and sees the broad picture all the time. Your imagination and vision frequently lead to new things being invented and discovered. These characteristics need an entrepreneur to physically shape his ideas and ambitions. The link between apparently unconnected events or situations is one element of creativity. Companies typically come up with solutions that summarize other issues. They are going to return items to new sectors to the market. In order for their ideas to come into effect, they must also be ready to move out of their comfort zone. These inventions sometimes lead to new technology and progress that can make industry breakthroughs.

7. Determining

Businessmen are not hindered by their losses. They see failure as a chance to succeed. They want to succeed in all their efforts and strive again until they do. They want to succeed. There is no belief that successful entrepreneurs can achieve things. The successful entrepreneur, therefore, has the tenacity to pursue all business ups and downs to attain his objectives and aspirations.

8. The ability of strong people

The contractor has great communication abilities that encourage the staff and market the product. The majority of successful business people are able to encourage their staff to develop their firm globally. They are particularly adept at emphasizing the advantages of all situations and helping others succeed.

9. Strong ethics of work

Successful contractors are always ready to make the effort they need. They are leaders, especially in the sense of urgency and responsibility, who set an important example for others. Often the successful contractor is the first person and the last person to leave the workplace. They will come to ensure that a result fulfils their expectations throughout their days off. Your mind is always at work, whether in or out of the place of employment.

10. Passion

A successful entrepreneur's enthusiasm is one of the most crucial traits. You love your work truly. You are prepared to put the company into that additional hour since it offers them a delight that goes beyond money. The effective contractor will always read and explore ways of improving the business. You are ready to spend your time and effort learning new techniques or apps to remain ahead of your rivals. They ensure that they always learn new things about their business to stay up with and be as effective as possible with new advancements.

Successful businessmen want to see what the view is on top of the mountain of business. They want to go deeper once they see it. They know how to talk to their employees, and their businesses soar as a result.

Product selection

Selection of the product: - • Selection of the product is the process in which the retailer selects the product form or material according to the market need. Product Selection Terms included: -

- Material.
- Forms.
- Color
- Price

Choosing the right product or service may be viewed as the key building element for each company.

Products are actually the most significant and apparent initial encounters with purchasers, i.e., end customers, in the firm. The psychological signals of personal characteristics, goals and strategic approaches are characterised by Customer's physical character of objects. This means that the most likely consumer shapes the thoughts and perspectives of the contractor.

Selection factors for the product

Offering- Demand gap

To a significant extent, the magnitude and scope of the possible and unfulfilled market demand that is the basis of business opportunity will determine the necessity to settle for a certain product.

One of the guiding principles in building a template of product selection criteria is that the product with the greatest frequency of need/demand is more likely to have success. Existing demand (a market) for the selected product must be clearly defined.

Financing Another significant factor when selecting an allowed method of selection is the quantity of the money that may be obtained. Sufficient cash is necessary for the pre-launch of the selected product such as development, manufacture, promotion, marketing and distribution.

Access to starting materials and availability

Product differences need various starting ingredients. Core management choices include factors such as the source of the resources, the quality and the amount of the raw materials to be attained. Is it possible to supply enough raw materials on a continuous basis? Where are the raw material locations required? They are accessible? Are they available?

Technical reasons

In the area of product selection undertakings, the product route carries a lot of weight. The choices made for a given product may also ensure that new equipment has been acquired or the gear utilised has been restructured. It is also technically appropriate for the user to consider the product.

Responsibility for profit/marketability

As is typically the case, the product will be picked that satisfies the requirement for optimal returns. The product should also be marketed as an essential feature.

Qualified and qualified staff

Continuing manufacturing and marketing will demand qualified employees. By decreasing waste, the costs connected with production must be reduced to a lowest level.

Policies and purposes of government

These criteria for product selection typically go beyond the control of the contractor. The policy guidelines of the government on the economy and trade generally benefit from national interests throughout time that may or may not contradict the company goals. Standard worldwide procedures advise the identification of a number of criteria for the selection of products. Each criterion may be assigned scores to produce an objective assessment.

Selection of products and process criteria

- **Acceptance of products**

Open market product testing might take a long time to discover the underlying problems of certain goods. This criterion is highly essential in the selection of entrepreneurial items. The acceptability level of the product on the market is linked to the extent to which it will be successful.

However, it is only through performing research that we are able to determine how well a product is received on the market.

Production costs

Production costs are part of the selection criterion in the company for a product. Businesses must develop items that allow for significant profit margins and so reduce manufacturing costs while boosting potential earnings.

Production costs thus play an essential role for businesses in product selection. Only goods are picked with the largest profit margin.

Pre-facility Study conducting

This indicates that a feasibility study should usually be carried out before a product is picked in entrepreneurship. However, a pre-study is done before this is done to show how the product is to function on the open market. A feasibility study evaluates the performance or feasibility of the product on the market. This resembles acceptance of the goods. This enables the contractor to choose the product that is most widely accepted on the open market.

The product's future

The future of the product makes an important contribution to the quality of the product rates. Consequently, the issues about the degree of demand for the product, acceptation of the product at the fixed price, the feasibility of the product and margins for substantial benefits must receive crucial answers. A product with a broad demand and excellent profit margins is most likely to be picked compared to the product with lower prospects.

Does a need or a desire satisfy it?

Two forces drive consumers; necessities and desires. Needs are needs; therefore their desire is more than just items that fulfil their want. You want the low-cost to the highly costly. Whatever the case, it is quite vital to know which product category is covered and constitutes an important factor for choosing a product in an enterprise.

Edge Giving Products

When picking enterprise goods, the ability to select items with an advantage against similar products is a key consideration. The market for current items similar to the products offered for sale is usually reviewed before the selection of the products. Therefore, it may be helpful to be critical of your product, so that only the finest items are chosen.

Strategy for pricing

The pricing of such a product has to be properly analysed before a product is picked in an enterprise.

Some items, although desired, are not profitable, as production costs may be considerable.

Consequently, a price strategy focusing on the product's profit potential will contribute to the product's performance. In that instance, the product meets the customer's demands while fulfilling the entrepreneur's profit expectations.

The factors used to pick a product in business are various and demand experience and a careful eye. A marketing consultant's services are also required to give valuable insights on selecting entrepreneurial items.

What are the expenses of capital?

Capital costs are those monies which are used to acquire, enhance or maintain a company's long-term assets in order to increase the company's efficiency and capacity. Long-term asset typically is tangible, fixed, not-consumable and has a valuable life of more than one accounting period. property, equipment or infrastructure In addition, the purchasing of items such as new equipment, machinery, soil, plant or buildings, furniture and applied equipment, business vehicles, software or immaterial items such as a patent or licences are part of the expenses for capital, which are also called Capex or expenses for capital expenses.

Cash flow statements include the spending amounts for an accounting period. In the short- and long-term financial status of a company, capital expenditures often have a considerable impact. Capex smart selections are so crucial for a company's financial health. Many firms generally aim to keep their past capital expenditure levels to convince investors that the company's management continues to invest in business growth.

Example of capital costs

Below is an accounting illustration of Amazon's 2015, 2016 and 2017 capital expenditure.

CONSOLIDATED STATEMENTS OF CASH FLOWS
(in millions)

	Year Ended December 31,		
	2015	2016	2017
CASH AND CASH EQUIVALENTS, BEGINNING OF PERIOD	$ 14,557	$ 15,890	$ 19,334
OPERATING ACTIVITIES:			
Net income	596	2,371	3,033
Adjustments to reconcile net income to net cash from operating activities:			
Depreciation of property and equipment, including internal-use software and website development, and other amortization, including capitalized content costs	6,281	8,116	11,478
Stock-based compensation	2,119	2,975	4,215
Other operating expense, net	155	160	202
Other expense (income), net	250	(20)	(292)
Deferred income taxes	81	(246)	(29)
Changes in operating assets and liabilities:			
Inventories	(2,187)	(1,426)	(3,583)
Accounts receivable, net and other	(1,755)	(3,367)	(4,786)
Accounts payable	4,294	5,030	7,175
Accrued expenses and other	913	1,724	283
Unearned revenue	1,292	1,955	738
Net cash provided by (used in) operating activities	12,039	17,272	18,434
INVESTING ACTIVITIES:			
Purchases of property and equipment, including internal-use software and website development	(5,387)	(7,804)	(11,955)
Proceeds from property and equipment incentives	798	1,067	1,897
Acquisitions, net of cash acquired, and other	(795)	(116)	(13,972)
Sales and maturities of marketable securities	3,025	4,733	9,988
Purchases of marketable securities	(4,091)	(7,756)	(13,777)
Net cash provided by (used in) investing activities	(6,450)	(9,876)	(27,819)

Accounting illustration of Amazon's 2015, 2016 and 2017 capital expenditure

What Amazon list in their cash flow statement is its capital spending for the periods: "Purchases of properties and devices including in-house software and website development." These investments are shown as negative amounts in the cash flow statement (cash outflows), therefore $11,955 million were invested by the firm in 2017.

Key takeovers

Capital expenses are money spent to purchase, enhance or proliferate fixed assets for one or more years in an organization and for a useful life. Such assets include property, facilities and infrastructure. In general, capital investment takes two different forms: acquisition and expansion expenditure.

Due to their significant initial costs, irreversibility and long-term impacts, choices on capital spending are highly important to a company. Consequently, capital expenditure budgeting should be planned and implemented carefully and effectively.

Capital spending challenges

Although decisions on capital spending are highly essential, they add extra complexity:

1. Issues of measurement

It may be extremely hard to identify, measure, and estimate the cost of capital investment.

2. Unforeseeable

Organizations investing heavily in capital assets aim to get predictable results. Such results are however not guaranteed and there might be losses. There is generally much ambiguity in the costs and benefit of capital investment choices. Sometimes even the greatest forecasts are wrong. When planning finance, companies have to bear the risk of mitigating future losses, even if they cannot be eliminated.

3. Spreading Temporary

Cost, as well as capital expenditure advantages, are often extended for both industrial and infrastructural projects over a reasonably lengthy period of time. Such a time distribution leads to issues in estimating the discount rate and setting equivalents.

Efficient budgeting of capital expenditure

Major capital projects with large sums of money and capital expenses can easily be disregarded if maladministrator and end up costing a company a lot of money. However, this does not have to be the case with efficient preparation, the proper tools and competent project management. Here are some of the techniques to make capital expenditure budgeting efficient.

1. Before you start to structure

Before starting, the budgets for capital expenditure need to be well prepared. They may be out of control otherwise. You need to find the project scope, develop realistic timelines, and ensure the complete plan is reviewed and endorsed before a project is initiated. You should consider at this point about how many internal resources, including personnel, materials, money and services, the project will require. You should delve into the project in greater depth to have a more realistic budget.

2. Long-term thinking

You have to determine if you are buying the assets under the loan or set aside current money for purchase at the start of your capital expenses project. Saving money for the purchase typically means you must wait a long before you obtain the property you need. Borrowing money, however, may lead to greater debt and also may lead to issues with your capacity to borrow. Both options might be excellent for your business and various selections for various tasks may be necessary.

3. Use Good software for budgeting

From the start of the project, a dependable, realistic budget management programme should be selected. The sort of budgeting software you pick will rely on project scope, programme speed and mistake risk.

4. Accurate data collection

If you want to run capital projects efficiently, accurate data is highly important. You have to collect accurate information to build a realistic budget and provide meaningful reports.

Capital Spending Importance

Decisions on how much to invest in the capital expenditure of a company may frequently be highly important. For the following reasons, they are important:

1. Long-term consequences

The impact of decisions on capital spending normally stretches to the future. The existing spectrum of production or production operations is mostly a result of prior investment on capital. Likewise, the present capital expenditure decisions will have a big effect on the company's future operations.

2. Irreversion

It is generally difficult to reverse capital investment without losses from the firm. Most capital equipment forms are adapted to the specifications and demands of particular companies. In general, the market is quite weak for equipment utilized.

3. High start-up costs

In particular for firms in areas such as production, production, production, telecom, utility companies and oil exploration, capital investment is usually highly costly. The possibility of delivering long-term advantages is capital expenditures in physical properties such as buildings, equipment or property, but will initially need a massive monetary expense and considerably larger than ordinary operational expenses. With increasing technology, the cost of capital is likewise growing.

4. Dismissal.

An initial rise in the organization's asset accounts is associated with capital expenses. Once the capital assets are placed into operation, however, depreciation occurs and their value decreases over the whole lifetime.

Registration procedures for the company

1. Registration procedure for a new company

On receipt of a company request for registration of their companies, on their letterhead asking Controller of Shops. In a standard format No.1(A), the Corporate Registration Section (FRS), asks them to provide information about the company. On receipt of information. Where a company satisfies the eligibility requirements, Rs.500/- will be requested as an initial payment for issuing the video form Standard Format Number 1 (B). The video standard format application.

price shall not be paid by companies registered with NSIC (B). Companies registered with NSIC shall not pay a charge for video Standard Format applications ii) When officially submitted by the company, when the application forms are received. If any are identified by letter in standard format No 2 FRS and inadequacies will be examined.

The company has provided all papers thereafter. The bankers of the enterprise will get information on the financial situation of the company by sending a private letter to the Standards Format No. 3.

The DGS&D Production Unit of the Zone Rly will get confirmation confidentially, if the company registers with NSIC, from the Agency that registered the company for group details. Class and company performance report by Standard Format No. 4. (v) In the event that the firm is not registered with any of the agencies, a COS Officer will be appointed to visit the premises of that company. For companies outside the station. SEC Railway Stores Branch's closest officer will be appointed. The HQ officer will usually give a report on the company's technical competence and financial capacity to the Officer who works with the business group required by the firm. When the inspection report is received. The FRS will fill in the Standard Format No. 5 and receive recommendations of the purchasing agent involved (JAF/SG) on the allocation and subsequent case of the COS decision about allocation of category and group of companies. FRS will then submit cases (s). (vi) The company will not be inspected if the company is registered at any other Zonal Rly/ Rly Manufacturing Unit or NSIC or DGS&D. The format no. file must be placed for the suggestion of the JAG/SG agents, who deal with the trade group. The matter will thereafter be put forward for COS decisions on class and trade group allocation (s).

In a standard Format No.6 with various terms and conditions, the company shall submit the submission of a weekly store bulletin as appropriate by procedure as soon as COS agrees to authorize registrations, and the company shall be requested. Initially, the registration time is for TWO YEARS and renewal is assessed for the performance.

Partnership Registration

There is no time constraint as such for registering a company under India Partnership Act 1932. The company can be registered on or after the date it is entered. The fees and fines necessary should be paid. The registration method is as follows:

1]Application on the required form to the company registrar (Form A). This facility is currently even available online. Such a request must contain some fundamental company data, such,

Partnership name

- Partnership name and address
- Place and location (head office/branch address)
- Duration of the partner
- Partner membership dates
- Date of start of business
- Partnership starts dates

2] The registrar must complete the properly signed copy of the Partnership Deed (which includes all terms and conditions)

3] The required fees and stamp duties are paid/deposited.

4] The company shall be entered in the records after the registrar accepts the application. And a certificate of incorporation will also be issued.

The registration procedure is done and the company is recognized legally.

Methods of import

The import and export operations often include the assuring that products are licensed and complied with before the delivery, transport and storage arrangements for goods after the unloading and customs clearance, as well as the payment of taxes before goods are delivered.

The stages required in importing products are outlined below.

1. Get IEC

Every firm must first have an import code (IEC) number from the Regional Joint DGFT before importing from India. The IEC is a life-long merchant registration necessary for customs clearance, shipment shipping and money sending or receiving in foreign monies.

It takes around 10-15 days to get IEC registration.

2. Ensure legal conformity with various trade legislation

After the IEC is allotted, companies are entitled to import products in accordance with Section 11 of the Customs Act (1962), the Law on Foreign Trade (1992) and the Foreign Trade Policy (2015-20).

However, some products — as proclaimed and communicated by the Government, limited, channeled or forbidden — require DGFT and the Federal Government's extra permits and licenses.

3. Contract permits to import

To establish if a licence is necessary in order to import a certain commodity or service, the importer has to categories the product, using a harmonized code system or ITC (HS) classification to identify the Indian Trading Clarification.

ITC (HS) is India's leading classification technique for trade and export activities. The ITC-HS code provided by the DGFT represents an 8-digit alphanumerical code of a class and class of products that permits the importer to comply with the rules on the items.

A general or special license may be an import license. Goods can be imported from any nation with a general license, whereas a particular license or a specific one allows imports from certain countries only.

Import licenses shall be utilized in import clearances, renewables, usually for 24 months for capital items or for 18 months for the components, consumables and replacement parts of raw materials.

4. File Entry Bill and other customs clearance completion papers

Importers must submit import declarations using a permanent account number (PAN) based business identification number on their mandated letters of entry after acquiring importation licenses (BIN), In accordance with Article 46 of the Customs Act (1962).

A letter of entry must provide information on the exact kind, number and value of the commodities arriving in the nation or coming into the country.

If the items are cleared by means of Electronic Data Interchange (EDI), the computer system will not produce a formal Bill of entry. However, after prescribing details necessary to complete the entry for customs clearance, the importer must file a cargo declaration.

If the Bill of Income is submitted without EDI, it is essential that the importer submits supporting papers which include the certificate of origin, the inspection certificate, the exchange bill, the list of invoices for commercial cum-packing, etc.

The customs officers should analyse and evaluate information provided in the entrance letter when the products are sent, and compare them with the things imported. Where there are no abnormalities, the officials issue a 'transfer order' which permits the replacement from customs of the items imported.

5. Determine duty rate of import for goods clearing

As set down in the first schedule of the Customs Tariff Act 1975, India charges basic customs taxes on the imported products together with other tariffs, including anti-dumping, safeguard and social welfare surcharges.

Furthermore, under the new GST system the government imposes an integrated goods and services tax (IGST). The IGST rates shall be based on the categorization of the products imported under the schedules issued under Section 5 of the IGST Act (2017).

Methods of export

As with imports, an export planning firm must receive an IEC number from the regional DGFT unit. The exporter must verify after getting the IEC that all legal compliance is complied with according to various commercial legislation.

In addition, the exporter must verify if a license to export is necessary, and thus apply to the DGFT for the license.

The Indian Chamber of Commerce (ICC) must also be registered by the exporter who issuing the Non-Preferential Certificates of Provenance certifying the origin of the exported products in India. Documents for import and export. Companies are needed in India to file a set of export and import paperwork. These include trade documents - those between buyer and seller and regulatory documents dealing with different regulatory, such as customs and excise authorities, license agencies, and export promotion agencies that support export-import benefits. export subsidies are also exchanged. For importing and exporting activities, the Foreign Trade Policy 2015-2020 specifies the following business papers.

- Lading bill or bill of flights;
- Cum packing list commercial invoice;
- Shipment bill, export bill or entrance bill (for imports).

• Further papers such as certificate of origin and certificate of inspection may be requested as appropriate.

Important documentation includes:

• GST (GSTR 1 and GSTR2) return forms;

• GSTR form reimbursement;

• Declaration of Exchange Control;

• Certificate of bank implementation;

• Cum Certificate of Registration (RCMC)

Sales Tax

The value of a product that is charged on the exchange or purchase point and is indirect is always a proportion of the Sale Tax. Retail, manufacturing, wholesale, usage and value-added tax are the different types of sales tax (VAT).

What is the Tax on Sales?

Sales tax is a tax form paid for the sale of goods and services by a government entity. The Sales Tax is an indirect tax that is typically imposed as a percentage of the value of the product at the moment of purchase or exchange of specified taxable products. The sales tax depends on the government and the laws implemented by it, which is usually straightforward to compute and collect. Simply put, the sales tax is a further sum paid for products or services.

Sales tax types

The notion of sales tax is based on governments' guiding principles, although in most nations, universal sales taxes apply. The following are the many forms of sales tax.

sales tax

Detail sales tax

This is the retail products tax and is paid directly by the end-user.

Sales tax for manufacturers

The makers of specific products are charged this tax.

Sales Tax This tax is imposed on persons who sell/sell manufactured items in wholesale.

Tax on use This is a tax on products acquired without a selling tax on the consumer (generally from vendors who are not under the tax jurisdiction).

• Value Added Tax VAT is a surcharge applied by some governments on all the sales.

Conventional or retail sales taxes shall be collected on sales to the final customer of the good and shall be charged whenever the item is sold. No tax is payable for sales to companies afterwards reselling the products. A non-end-user buyer is generally given by the taxation authority with a 'resale Certificate,' which is necessary at the time of the purchase to present a seller with the certificate (or ID) coupled with a statement indicating the product is to be sold. Any item sold without such a certificate to customers under the competence of the taxation authorities else charges the tax.

Additional forms of sales tax or comparable taxes:

• Sales tax of manufacturers, tax on sales by producers and producers of tangible personal property

• wholesaling sales tax, wholesale sales tax on personal physical goods when prepared for sale or delivery to end users and consumers in form, packed and labelled

sales retail, tax on sales to consumers and industrial users of tangible personal property

Gross revenue tax, charged for all sales of a company. Their 'cascada' or 'pyramid' effect has been criticized, which taxes an item over time as the item moves from manufacture to ultimate retail sales.

excise duties, generally placed on the manufacturer, or wholesaler instead of retailers, on a restricted range of items, such as gasoline or alcohol.

Tax of use levied on the consumer of products bought without a sales tax typically things bought by a vendor not subject to the taxing authority's jurisdiction (such as a vendor in another state). Use taxes are generally imposed by sales tax states, although usually just for big products, such as cars and boats.

Currency exchange tax, securities trading tax.

Tax added value (Value Added Tax), which taxes all sales, preventing a resale certificate system that is necessary. Cascading by tax should be avoided by applying the tax solely to the difference ("value added") between the price paid by the first buyer and the price paid by the next buyer of the same item.

FairTax, a federal sales tax, suggested as a substitute for US tax.

Tax on sales, comparable to a sales tax, but applicable as an indirect tax for mid- and perhaps capital items.

Most of the nations in the world have national, state, county or local government sales or value-added taxes on all or more of them.

Countries in Western Europe have some of the highest value added taxes, particularly in Scandinavia. Hungary's highest VAT is 26.0 per 100, however the rate is in some circumstances decreased for food, art, literature and news media. Norway, Denmark and Sweden have higher VATs of 25 percent. There are several levels of government in certain areas in the United States that each need a sales tax. In Chicago, for instance, IL is 10.25% consisting of a state of 6.25%; a city of 1.25%; a county of 1.75%; and a regional transit authority of 1%. Chicago also has a 1 per cent food and beverage tax on the Metropolitan Pier and Exposure Authority (which means eating out is taxed at 11.25 percent).

For the Louisianan state of Baton Rouge, a tax of 9.45% is 4.45%, and 5% is local. It is 9.5 per cent in Los Angeles, a state of 7.25 per cent and a county of 2.25 per cent.

Sales taxes consist of different local, state and county tax in California. The "privilege of selling material personal property at the shop" is "imposed on all retailer" Strictly, only the retailer is liable for paying the tax; the customer just refunds the shop through a contractual arrangement, if a merchant adds this tax to the purchase price. If customers buy products from the outside State (the supplier does not owe taxes to California in this situation), the consumer is obliged to pay a "use tax" equivalent to the sales tax. Use tax shall be charged in this state on tangible personal property for "storage of, use of or other consumption." Consumers must report these purchases in the same file as their yearly government revenue tax, although this is unusual for them. The non-state acquisition of vehicles is an exception. The state collects use tax as part of California's car registration process.

The trend was to substitute more generally based value-added tax for conventional sales taxes. Value-added taxes are expected to represent 20% of tax income worldwide, and more than 140 nations have been accepted. The US is currently one of the few nations with traditional sales taxes.

Preparation of the project report

Many kinds of projects exist. You may learn the procedures and apply them to your own project with a single example. For instance, in your town, you must open a large retail business. You invest your own funds for this purpose. However, you don't have enough money. You need a bank loan; this is your project. To do so, through your project report, you must present your project. The major actions are then taken.

Following are its main steps:

1.Writing the Top Report Proposal

Through your project report, you must make clear proposals to the bank. You might write, I have my own commercial property with Rs. 50,00,000 of that worth. I invest in the retail shop the same way. I got Rs. 10,00,000 except this. However, that is not enough. To build a showroom and increase stocks, I need Rs. 40,00,000 in the huge shop. For, I'm offering this. You may either offer me a loan or you can become a 40 percent partner of my company. You're the bank. You're bank. You may also establish the showroom or offer me the present market rate loan. I'm ready to provide you security property registry.

2. Write the project's main goals

You should express the main objective of the project after drafting a proposal. You might state, for instance, that your objective is to offer essential items at extremely low prices to end customers.

3. Write the project's overall budget

The budget cost for each element of your proposal must be written in this area. You must create the store building, for instance. Write down the builders' estimated cost. The actual builder's market cost is Rs. 100 per square feet, for example, and you may make a budget correctly. The cost per square feeder is Rs. 100. This requires you to write out the budget for building materials. Except that, the budget of the items you have to show in this store must also be shown.

4. Display employee data that works in the project

The details of all employees who work on the same project must be included.

5. Report Highlight

If your project becomes apparent, you should outline the expected sales and revenues.

6. Recommendations whole report

You may write his suggestions in the same project report if your CA produces your report. He will check your project and then provide recommendations for that purpose. He can create a statement and balance sheet on your intended revenue. He will also make sure you follow various regulations that relate to your project. It calculates the estimated accounting ratios, such as the debt-to-equity ratio and the present ratio.

CHAPTER IV

Financial Management-Money Banking,International Trade,Foreign Exchange, Various Taxes,Types Of Accounts And Books,Trial Balance, Financial Accounts.

Introduction

Financial management is the planning, organization, management, and control of financial operations, for instance, the purchase and use of the company's finances. It indicates that general management concepts are applied to the company's financial resources.

In any business, financial management is an essential function. It is the planning, organization, management, and supervision of financial resources in order to fulfill corporate objectives. It is an ideal practice to manage an organization's financial operations such as money procurement, use of funds, accounting, payments, risk assessment and everything else relating to money. There are various alternatives to handle your money, such as operating your own business, employing a full-time worker, hiring a part-time accountant or a third party to manage all the financial operations for you, e.g., a Chartered Accountant.

- **Brief idea of Money banking**

When securities are purchased or sold, financial markets produce prices. Whenever loans are made to companies or individuals, financial institutions value financial assets. Pricing and appraisal of financial assets are therefore central to the financial market. One of our aims is to relate the behaviour of the prices of assets, including stocks and bonds, with the economic performance in general and to the performance of financial and market institutions.

First of all, however. What does money, banking and financial markets imply, precisely? The money in the money, banking and financial markets not only refers to the greenbacks that we spend, but to the monetary system in more general terms. As you understand, money plays an important part in economic performance. It permits not just trade between millions of economic participants, but is the primary method by which central banks try to affect aggregate economic activity, which includes economic growth, employment and inflation. Banks and other financial intermediaries are concerned with money, banking and financial markets. A financial intermediary is an entity that redeploys the cash by investing in financial assets from a group of investors Banks are the main custodian of the financial supply of the economy, providing major sources of cash for consumers and companies, in cooperation with other financial intermediaries. The monetary, banking and financial markets refer to those marketplaces in which financial assets can be exchanged. For people having over finances for purchasing assets such as stock and bonds issued by others in need of funds, financial markets provide a method. In addition, financial markets give stock and bond prices to ensure that we know whether or not we should conceal or praise recent acquisitions.

An Overview

• Modern economic money is sometimes considered a lubricant that grades economic activity wheels. Without money, it would be impossibly impossible to transact our everyday economic routine and save and invest almost in full-time occupations.

But money is more than simply a lubricant that makes the economy function smoothly. The financial institutions and markets also play an important role in shaping their economic behaviour and their success. In particular, changes in money and credit supply may influence the growth of the economy, the number of jobs and inflation, which can, in turn, influence the value of financial assets owned by individuals and organisations.

•In the economy, banks play a crucial role. Banks give people and companies the opportunity to invest their cash to earn minimal risk interest.

By creating loans, banks in turn redistribute these funds. In this context, the banks are significantly comparable to other financial intermediaries, for example financing firms and insurance companies, which likewise purchase and transfer cash from individuals and enterprises to others. Banks are especially well suited, as are financing firms and life insurance companies, to participate in the most difficult forms of financial investment, namely loans to individuals and small organisations.

Banking and Financial Institutions

• Banks and other financial institutions are what make financial markets work. Financial intermediaries

• institutions that take money from savings and loans from people · banks · Institutions that accept deposits and loans — are companies that are included as banks of business, savings and credit, and other banks that are not capable of shifting funds from the financial markets to people with productive investment opportunities.

• Other Financial Institutions — Insurance, Finance, Pension, mutual and investment banks • Financial innovation — especially the emergence of the age of information and e-finance

Banks are key international commerce facilitators. They guarantee payment for roughly a fifth of global commerce, in addition to the provision of liquidity. Therefore, in international business, the banking sector plays an essential role. Today, nearly all banks have created collaborative partnerships in other nations to better serve their international business community and have built corresponding bank ties with banks. Banks play an important part in creating a trust connection in international markets between purchasing and selling agents. Local banks have external intermediate banks that help to carry out international payments, thereby receiving and paying local individuals for products and services.

The financial framework and the tools required for conducting commercial transactions between overseas purchasers or sellers play a key role in foreign commerce. Banks manage the movement of papers and money for safety and transparency. The sellers (exporters) will want to be assured of payment by buyers (importers) of products from abroad, and one would need as a buyer assurance of compliance with all terms, conditions and conditions under the buying agreement. This therefore requires the banks to conclude an agreement and to act as a middleman between the importer and the exporter.

Money banking significance

Bond Market is a method for which financial securities buyers and sellers are trading in a financial debt claim for cash supplied to another individual for a set time period at a predetermined interest rate. In order to determine the interest rate, bonds are economic indications regarding the loan from private and government companies.

Interest rate is the cost of borrowing or of leasing money, or the cost not to use one's own money. The rates of interest vary with the lending duration. It is lower for long-term credit. It's almost normal for medium-term lending but generally is higher than average for short-term lending. The economy is derived from the interest rates through an increase or decrease in the financial supply.

Demand for Money Interest Rate, Supply for Money

When the central bank wishes to limit inflation by a reduction in the economic money supply, it raises the interest rate, resulting in low money demand. However, this component generates poor investment, resulting in unemployment and falling domestic output.

On the other hand, it allows trade banks to advance loans at a cheap interest rate, thereby increasing their money supply in the economy when the central bank wishes to stimulate the economy and business activity in their nation. People have many more investing options at this time, but they have little or no money. With the drop in the interest rate and more money supplies, consumers rush towards money consumption for various items and services, which promotes inflation with a decrease in interest rates, causing the overall level of prices to climb.

Stock Market:

Stock Market is a location where stocks of different businesses (Common stock, share of the cooperationists earnings and assets are traded for the security of money supplied to the corporation by an individual investor). Prices are stated in a company's market demand and share supply. In line with the regulations, policies and commitments which the managers ensure of each shareholder, a high share price shows that corporate activities are performed.

Foreign exchange market:

FEM is where currencies are traded from nation to country (say PKR) (say US$). Foreign exchange has a significant influence on every country's economic condition. When Pakistan exports less in other nations than USD 1 = 52 PKR, it is because Pakistani items are cheaper for international buyers than USD 1 = PKR 86 as the Pakistani exports are less than USD 1 in Pakistan.

International trade

The world in which we live and live shapes our daily life. We are involved in the global economy almost every time we buy or sell. Complete items and their parts are available from all over the world in our shop shelves. The most important foreign commerce is buying and selling industrial appliances, consumer items, petroleum and agricultural products. One-fifth of the world's commerce comprises services such as banking, insurance, transport, telecommunications, technology and tourism.

You will have an influence on global commerce if you can go to a store and find Costa Rican bananas, Brazilian coffee and a bottle of South African wine.

International commerce helps nations, otherwise not locally available, to extend market access and access products and services. The market is more competitive as a result of foreign commerce. In the final analysis, this gives the consumer more competitiveness and a cheaper product.

- International commerce provides consumers and nations with the chance to be exposed to goods and services which are not accessible or are more expensive domestically in their own country, and the interchange of goods and services across countries is a key feature. Political economists like Adam Smith and David Ricardo have early recognised the significance of international commerce.
- However, others believe that international trade may actually be harmful to smaller nations and put them at a greater disadvantage in the global arena.

Imports and Exports

An export is a product sold to the world market, whereas an import is a product purchased from the world market. The balance of payments of a country must account for imports and exports in the current account section.

Global commerce enables rich countries to utilise their resources more efficiently, including labour, technology and money. The various countries have various assets and natural resources: land, labour, capital, technology and so on. In other words, it makes it possible for some nations to make the same item more effectively and at a lower cost. They may thus sell it cheaper than others. When a country is unable to manufacture an item effectively, it may be achieved through trade with another country. This is referred to as an international trade specialty.

England and Portugal have, for example, benefitted historically through specialisation and commerce based on their comparative advantages. Portugal has many wine yards and can produce wine at a low price, whereas England can produce fabric more cheaply, given its sheep pastures. Every country would finally realise these truths and cease trying to make the product more expensive to produce locally to encourage commerce. In reality, over time, British wine came to an end, with Portugal stopping textile production. Both nations realised that they had the advantage to cease making these products at home and trade with each other instead.

Foreign Exchange

Foreign exchange (Forex or FX) is a conversion at a certain rate known as the foreign exchange rate of one currency to another. Conversion rates for nearly all currencies float continually due to the dynamics of supply and demand on the market. Worldwide, the dollar, euro, Japanese yen, British pound and Australian dollars are the most traded currencies. The US dollar continues to be the major currency for over 87% of the total daily value.

Factors Affecting Currency Value

A market force based on commerce, investment, tourism and geopolitical hazard will be used as the worth of any given currency. For example, a visitor must pay for products and services using the host nation's currency each time a country visits. A visitor must thus convert his country's money for the local currency. This sort of currency exchange is one of the causes demanding a certain currency.

The Foreign Exchange Market

- Devises where funds are converted from one currency to another
- FDR price is the price of one currency in respect of another currency
- Devises sets the devises rate

The impact of inflation on foreign exchange rates

Inflation may have a significant influence on the value of the foreign exchange and currencies of a country. Although inflation is only one element of many, the most likely negative effect on value and foreign-exchange rates of a currency are inflation. A very low inflation rate does not ensure a good exchange rate, but it is quite probable that an exceptionally high inflation rate will have a bad effect.

There is also a strong relationship between inflation and interest rates, which can impact exchange rates. For currency-issuing countries, the link between interest rates and inflation is complicated and frequently difficult to handle. Low-interest rates stimulate consumer expenditure and growth, typically influencing monetary value positively. Inflation may occur, which is not always a poor result if consumer spending increases and the demand goes beyond supply. But, like with the higher interest rates, low-interest rates don't generally attract international investment. Higher rates of interest attract foreign investment that will likely raise currency demand.

Various taxes such as property

Taxes

A tax is a mandatory fee or financial charge levied by any government on an individual or an organization to collect revenue for public works providing the best facilities and infrastructure. The collected fund is then used to fund different public expenditure programs. If one fails to pay the taxes or refuse to contribute towards it will invite serious implications under the pre-defined law.

The Constitution of India gives the authority to governments to levy taxes in India under the Indian tax system. As per the directives of the Indian tax system, the government collects taxes from its citizens to generate income for undertaking public-works projects and improve the country's economic footprint.

The Indian tax system allows common taxpayers to plan their taxes and earn maximum tax-saving benefits. Additionally, if an individual invests money into any tax-saving instrument, there is a provision for tax exemption on the same. Let us understand the different types of taxes in India and their benefits in detail.

What are the Different Types of Taxes?

Mainly, there are two kinds of taxes defined under the Indian tax system, which get further sub-divided into other categories:

1. Direct taxes in India
2. Indirect taxes in India

Direct Tax

The definition of direct tax is hidden in its name which implies that this tax is paid directly to the government by the taxpayer

The general examples of this type of tax in India are Income Tax and Wealth Tax.

From the government's perspective, estimating tax earnings from direct taxes is relatively easy as it bears a direct correlation to the income or wealth of the registered taxpayers.

The Different Types of Direct Taxes In India

1. Income tax

The tax that gets levied on the annual income or the profits of an individual or an entity is Income Tax. Therefore, the Indian tax system recognizes both salaried and self-employed individuals who are earning an income, to be liable to pay income tax. Also, there is also a tax exemption limit of up to Rs.2.5 lakh per annum under the Indian tax system, given to individuals below 60 years of age.

2. Securities Transaction Tax

The securities transaction tax, as defined under the Indian tax system, gets levied on the stock market and securities trading. This tax is imposed on the price of the share and the traded securities traded on the ISE (Indian Stock Exchange).

Following are some other types of taxes that fall under the direct tax category:

1. Wealth Tax
2. Gift Tax
3. Estate Duty
4. Expenditure Tax
5. Fringe Benefit Tax

Indirect Tax

Indirect taxes are slightly different from direct taxes and the collection method is also a bit different. These taxes are consumption-based that are applied to goods or services when they are bought and sold.

The indirect tax payment is received by the government from the seller of goods/services.

The seller, in turn, passes the tax on to the end-user i.e. buyer of the good/service.

Thus the name indirect tax as the end-user of the good/service does not pay the tax directly to the government.

Some general examples of indirect tax include sales tax, Goods and Services Tax (GST), Value Added Tax (VAT), etc.

Indirect taxes in India

Taxes that get imposed on products and services when they are bought and sold are called indirect taxes in India. The sellers of the service or products collect these taxes under the Indian tax system. The tax gets levied as an addition to the original price of the product or service, which increases their cost. Following are the different types of indirect taxes in India.

Goods and Services Tax

Goods or Services Tax (GST) is a consumption tax imposed on services and goods supply and has completely replaced the indirect taxes in India. The Indian tax system stipulates that every stage of the goods production process and value-added services is under the obligation to pay GST.

The introduction of GST under the Indian tax system has resulted in the abolition of other kinds of indirect taxes in India and charges like Value Added Tax (VAT), OCTROI, Central Value Added Tax (CENVAT), and also custom and excise taxes.

Following are some other types of taxes that fall under the indirect tax category:

1. Securities Transaction Tax
2. Dividend Distribution Tax
3. Property Tax
4. Professional Tax
5. Entertainment Tax
6. Registration Fees, Stamp Duty, Transfer Tax
7. Education cess
8. Entry Tax
9. Road Tax and Toll Tax

Property Tax

Definition: Property tax is the annual amount paid by a land owner to the local government or the municipal corporation of his area. The property includes all tangible real estate property, his house, office building and the property he has rented to others.

Central government properties and vacant property are generally exempt. Property tax comprises taxes like lighting tax, water tax and drainage tax.

Types of Property

Property, in India is classified into four categories, which help the government estimate tax based on certain criteria. The different property divisions in the country are mentioned below.

Land – in its most basic form, without any construction or improvement.

Improvements made to land - this includes immovable manmade creations like buildings and godowns.

Personal property – This includes movable man-made objects like cranes, cars or buses.

Intangible property

Steps to Pay Property Tax Online

Step - 1:Log in to the official website of their municipality/city corporation.

Step - 2: Choose the tab indicating property tax and navigate to the payment option.

Step - 3: Choose the right form (either 4 or 5), based on the category under which an individual's property falls. These forms are used to determine if any changes have been made to a property in question.

Step - 4: Choose the assessment year. This is the year for which property tax needs to be calculated and paid. Most corporations provide an option to clear backlogs in property tax payment.

Step - 5: Individuals will then be required to fill in their property identification number and any other relevant document pertaining to their property (zone under which it falls, property type, etc.) including the owner's name.

Step - 6: Once all relevant information has been entered, individuals can choose the mode of payment, which could be credit/debit cards or internet banking.

Step - 7: Once payment is made individuals can take a printout of the challan for their reference.

Note: These are the basic steps involved in paying property tax online and could vary depending on the city/town corporation.

Calculation of Property Tax

The formula used for calculating property tax is given below:

Property tax = base value × built-up area × Age factor × type of building × category of use × floor factor.

Wealth Company Income, Excise Duty, Sales Tax.

Wealth Company Income

The two terms are related but they do not have the same meaning wealth is a stock concept. It is a large number of variable possessions while income is a flow of money.

Wealth – For individual people like you and me, it can be held

In a variety of forms:

- Saving is held in deposit accounts in banks.
- Possession of government and corporate bonds.
- Equity stakes in private companies, and ownership of shares issued by public companies (listed in stock markets).
- Money held in life assurance and occupational pension schemes.
- Property ownership.
- If the total net wealth of an individual, huf or company exceeds Rs 30 lakhs, on the valuation date, tax @1% will be leviable on the amount in excess of RS.30 lakhs. Every person whose net wealth exceeds such limit shall furnish a return of net wealth.

Income - This is the flow of money going to factors of production, and may include.

- Rent paid to the landlord.

- The wages and salaries of employees.

- State pension, tax credits, unemployment benefits, and other money paid in the form of welfare benefits to individuals or households.

-Dividends paid to shareholders, as well as interest paid to bank accounts and bondholders.

Wealth Tax in India

India's tax system involves many different types of taxes and one of them is wealth tax (a.k.a. net worth tax, capital tax, or equity tax). The government abolished the wealth tax as announced in the budget 2015. In its stead, the government decided to increase the surcharge levied on the 'super rich' class by 2% to 12%. Super rich are persons with incomes of Rs.1 crore or higher and companies that earn Rs.10 crores or higher. The abolition was a move to do away with the high costs of collection and also to simplify the existing tax structure thereby discouraging tax evasion.

Basic provisions

Following are the basic provisions of Wealth-tax Law which are to be kept in mind:

- Wealth-tax is levied on the following persons only:
- an individual;
- a Hindu undivided family (HUF); and
- a company.

Persons other than individuals, Hindu Undivided Families (HUFs) and companies are not liable to pay wealth tax. A partnership firm is not liable to wealth tax, but the assets of the partnership firm are charged to tax in the hands of the partners of the firm in the form of "Interest in partnership firm". In other words, a partnership firm is not liable to wealth tax, but the value of the assets held by the firm is to be ascertained and this value will be distributed amongst the partners of the firm and will be charged to tax in the hands of the partners. However, where a minor is admitted to the benefits of partnership in a firm, the value of the interest of such minor in the firm shall be included in the net wealth of the parent of the minor. Similarly, an association of persons (not being a co-operative housing society) is not liable to wealth tax, but the assets of the association of person are charged to tax in the hands of its members in the form of "Interest in partnership firm". Wealth tax is levied on the net wealth owned by a person on the valuation date, i.e., 31st March of every year. Wealth tax is levied at 1% on the net wealth in excess of Rs. 30,00,000

Wealth Tax Rules

Who does wealth tax apply to or who has to pay wealth tax and how is it applied?

The residential status of an individual was one of the key parameters to ascertain wealth tax liability. Resident Indians were liable to pay wealth tax on their global assets. However, non-resident Indians and foreigners were liable to pay wealth tax on their assets in India only. If a non-resident Indian returns to India, his assets would not be exempt from wealth tax. Assets acquired by NRIs within one year of their return are also exempt.

Assets that were covered under wealth tax:

Wealth tax was payable on assets such as real estate and gold. Assets such as shares, mutual funds and securities termed as 'productive assets', were exempt from wealth tax.

Yachts, aircraft and boats came under the purview of wealth tax.

While one residential home is exempt, more than one owns house would come under the purview of wealth tax. However, wealth tax is not applicable on a property if it is used for business or rented for 300 days in a year.

Tax is levied on the market price of a car, except when used in a car hiring business.

Gold, platinum and silver ornaments came under the purview of wealth tax. Also, wealth tax is applicable to cash-in-hand above Rs. 50,000.

If a taxpayer had to pay wealth tax, transferring his or her assets to the spouse would not result in evasion of the levy, since assets even if gifted, would be considered the property of the taxpayer.

How is a wealth tax calculated?

A wealth tax is typically a tax on a net worth (the difference between someone's assets and liabilities). For example, if somebody has $500,000 of assets and $300,000 of debt, that person's wealth (or net worth) is $200,000 and a 2% wealth tax would generate a $4,000 tax bill.

Estate taxes, gift taxes and inheritance taxes are examples of wealth taxes that are typically assessed once or infrequently.

A taxing authority might decide to assess a wealth tax annually, periodically or only when certain events occur, such as when somebody transfers wealth to someone else.

The taxing authority might also exempt certain assets or liabilities from the wealth tax, and it might apply different tax rates to different levels of wealth.

Calculating someone's wealth tax typically begins with determining the value of the person's assets and liabilities or debts. That can be tricky for assets such as houses, businesses, jewelry and other items.

Excise Duty

Excise duty refers to the taxes levied on the manufacture of goods within the country, as opposed to custom duty that is levied on goods coming from outside the country. Readers should note that GST has now subsumed a number of indirect taxes including excise duty. This means excise duty, technically, does not exist in India except on a few items such as liquor and petroleum. The information given below pertains to the functioning of Excise Duty in India before the implementation of GST regime.

Excise Duty is a form of indirect tax which is generally collected by a retailer or an intermediary from its consumers and then paid to the government. Although this duty is payable on manufacture of goods, it is usually payable when the goods are 'removed' from the place of production or from the warehouse for the purpose of sale. There is no requirement for the actual sale of the goods for imposing the excise duty because it is imposed on the manufacture of such goods. The Central Board of Excise and Customs (CBEC) is responsible for collecting excise duty.

Acts and Rules Governing Excise Duty in India

The legal framework around Excise Duty is majorly governed by the two acts-

Central Excise Act, 1944

Central Excise Tariff Act, 1985

The two acts underline the laws related to the levying of excise duty that extends to the whole of India.

The rates of Central Excise Duty are defined by the Central Excise Tariff Act, 1985. The Central Excise Act majorly provides the definitions related to excise while the Central Excise Tariff Act includes an elaborate schedule of excisable goods and the tariffs on them. The CBEC, which functions under the leadership of the Finance Minister, administers the levy of excise and custom laws in the country.

Types of Excise Duty in India

There are three types of excise duties in India-

Basic Excise Duty- Sometimes referred to as Central Value Added Tax (CENVAT), this type of excise duty is imposed on goods classified under the first schedule of the Central Excise Tariff Act, 1985. This duty is imposed under Sectio of the Central Excise Act, 1944 and levied on all excisable goods in the country except salt.

Additional Excise Duty- According to the Section 3 of the Additional Duties of Excise (Goods of Special Importance) Act, 1957, this duty is levied on goods listed in Schedule 1 of the given act. Such duty is levied on some specific goods and is charged by the central and state government as a substitute of the sales tax. The Additional Duties of Excise (Textiles and Textile Articles) Act, 1978 also provide for a similar legislation.

Special Excise Duty- This kind of duty is levied on special goods specified under the Second Schedule to the Central Excise Tariff Act, 1985.

Sales Tax

The indirect tax imposed on the selling and purchasing of goods within India is referred to as Sales Tax. It is an additional amount paid over and above the base value of the product being purchased. This tax, usually imposed on the seller by the government, enables the seller to recover the tax from the purchaser. It is usually charged from buyers at the point of purchase or the exchange of some specific goods and is chargeable at a certain percentage of the product value.

Sales Tax is levied by the Central Government as well as State Governments. It is decided by the Central Government basis its tax policies. State Sales Tax laws vary between states.

Types of Sales Tax

Though countries across geographies have their unique Sales Tax policies, there are certain standard types of sales taxes that are applicable to most countries. They are:

Wholesale Sales Tax – Tax levied on individuals dealing with the wholesale distribution of goods is referred to as Wholesale Sales Tax.

Manufacturers' Sales Tax – Tax charged on manufacturers of some specific goods is known as Manufacturers' Sales Tax.

Retail Sales Tax – Tax levied on the sale of retail goods and directly payable by the final consumer is called Retail Sales Tax.

Use Tax – This is a tax levied on the consumer for goods bought without paying sales tax. This usually holds true when goods are bought from vendors who are not a part of the tax jurisdiction.

Value Added Tax – An additional tax levied by some central governments on all purchases is called the Value Added Tax.

Finance Forecasting

Financial Forecasting is the process or processing, estimating, or predicting a business's future performance. With a financial prognosis, you try to predict how the business will look financially in the future.

Financial forecasting is a vital part of business planning that uses past financial performance and current conditions or trends to predict future company performance. In other words, financial forecasts are a tool by which businesses can set and meet goals.

Many factors can affect the level of confidence you have in your financial forecasts. However, they are always valuable indicators of whether your organization is moving in the right direction. Forecasts can be made on a weekly, monthly, quarterly or yearly basis, depending on the numbers that are being tracked—and they can address metrics such as sales, expenses, cost of goods sold, and profits.

What makes financial Forecasting important?

1. Financial Forecasting is a tool for entrepreneurs and CEOs to make better business decisions in a multitude of scenarios. It also helps with:
2. Convincing investors to finance a company
3. Setting objectives and budgets
4. When running a company, it's tempting to only look in the rear mirror by analyzing financial data from the past. But the result is that questions like the ones below will remain unanswered:
5. How will the future financial situation of my company look?
6. How much money can we payout to shareholders this year?
7. How much money can we generate this year to repay debts?
8. How long until all debts are repaid?
9. What will the organization's profitability and cash flow look like for the next six to eighteen months?
10. How can we achieve our financial objectives?

Types of Financial Forecasting

Quantitative forecasts

Quantitative forecasts use analyses of large quantities of historical data to identify trends and patterns. Quantitative forecasts are – generally speaking – less susceptible to skewing than speculative forecasts. However, if there isn't much historical data available, the quantitative method becomes less effective. That's why quantitative and speculative forecasts are often used in tandem.

Examples of quantitative forecasting methods are:

Pro-forma financial statements

Pro-forma financial statements mainly use the sales figures and expected costs of previous years as the basis for making forecasts. More about this later.

Time series analysis

The time series forecast is a popular quantitative forecasting technique that involves collecting data during a certain period in order to identify trends. Time-series analyses are one of the simplest ways to use and can be quite accurate, particularly in the short term.

Cause-effect method

In the Cause-effect method, the forecaster looks for cause-effect relationships of variables with other variables like changes in disposable income of consumers, level of consumer confidence, interest rates, unemployment, etc. This method uses time series from the past for many of the relevant variables based on which the forecast is created.

Qualitative forecasts

Speculation is something that's done based on intuition and experience. The human mind is able to see connections between events and understand the context in ways that computers can't. However, people are also prone to having certain biases that make it a challenge to process and analyses large quantities of data. Speculative forecasts are best used in small businesses with little or no historical data available.

Examples of qualitative forecasting methods are:

Expert opinions and visions

For this method, the opinions and key personnel from departments like production, sales, procurement, and operations are gathered to arrive at a forecast.

Reference forecasts

This method is about forecasting the outcomes of planned actions based on similar scenarios from other time periods or places. These forecasts are purely based on human judgement.

Delphi method

For the Delphi method, a series of questionnaires is created and filled out by a group of experts, independently from each other. After the results of the first questionnaire have been collected, a second one is created based on the results of the first. The second document is again presented to the

Experts are then asked to re-evaluate the answers they gave in the first questionnaire. This process will be repeated until the researchers arrive at a shared list of widely held opinions.

Consumer research

Companies often conduct market research among consumers. Data is collected via, for instance, phone calls, interviews, questionnaires, or sample tests. The enormous amount of information that is yielded by this is subjected to analyses in order to generate forecasts.

Scenario forecasts

In this method, the forecaster generates various results based on the outcomes of different scenarios. The management team has the final say about which is the most likely outcome of the many scenarios.

Three basic components of Financial Forecasting

Financial forecasting refers to creating certain financial statements. These statements are also called Pro-forma statements. Three statements are important when making financial prognoses. These are:

- Income statement
- Cash flow statement
- Pro-forma balance sheet

Some of these statements have to be filled out in the right order. The income statement, or profit-and-loss statement, tells you how much money comes in to the business, and how much goes out. The cash flow statement shows how the money is turned into a profit. The balance sheet helps to predict required payments, assets, and equity.

When these statements are accurate and complete, a business owner can make a financial forecast about how the organization will look over time.

Benefits of Financial Forecasting

Some of the benefits of financial forecasting include:

- Assess the success of your efforts to determine the long-term viability or value of an activity.
- Take control of your cash flow and purposefully direct your company.
- Develop benchmarks for use in future forecasts
- Perform contingency planning during challenging financial times
- Anticipate the impact of new expenses
- Identify financial problem areas and their causes

- Reduce financial risk
- Create an environment of certainty and stability
- Make future budgeting much easier

Steps for Producing a Financial Forecast

Determine the purpose of the forecast. Consider how it will be used, the degree of accuracy needed, factors that will come into play, and the time and effort that will be invested into creating the forecast.

Choose your forecast time frame.

Establish a method for producing the forecast.

Schedule team Huddles for gathering and analyzing data. A forecasting Huddle process that looks two or three months ahead is ideal.

Document the forecast and monitor the results. Use the results of the forecast to project cash from operations that can then become a critical element in a forward-looking cash flow report.

Repeat based on your forecasting time frame and analyze the effectiveness of your efforts.

Financial forecasting encourages employees to think about the future and how improvement in the execution of their daily tasks can have a positive impact on results. It helps people throughout the organization focus on a common goal.

Types of accounts & account books

All business establishments and taxpayers are required to keep a record of their day to day business transactions in order to know the result of their operations. The said record is referred to as "book of accounts".

Whenever a business establishment or taxpayer applies for certificate of registration (COR) with the BIR, it also required to register the book of accounts. Also, the books of account should also be registered annually on or before January 31 of each year.

Registration of book of accounts can be any of the following types:

Manual Books of Account

Manual books of account are the traditional journal, ledger and columnar books you can buy in the book and office supplies store. Recording in the manual books of account is handwritten. This is the most of popular type of book of account for small enterprises since it is less costly and easy to register with the BIR.

Loose-leaf Books of Account

Loose-leaf books of account are printed and bounded journals and ledgers. Recording can be done using Microsoft Excel.

Computerized Books of Account

A computerized book of account is an accounting program that facilitates efficient and fast record keeping.

Books of Accounts – Minimum Requirements

The type of books the business will maintain depends on many factors such as the size of the business and financial capacity. However, regardless of the type of book of accounts the company would maintain, below are the minimum requirement:

General Journal

The general journal is referred to as the book of original entry. It records the business transactions in order of date using the principle of "debit and credit".

General Ledger

The general ledger is referred to as the book of final entry. It summarized all the journal entries of an account to get the ending balances.

Cash Receipt Journal

Cash receipt journal is a special journal used to record cash sales and/or collection of receivables.

Cash Disbursement Journal

Cash disbursement journal is a special journal used to record cash payments of expenses and/or payables.

Sales Journal

Sales journal is a special journal used to record sales on credit (receivable from customers)

Purchase Journal

Purchase journal is a special journal used to record purchases on credit (payable to the supplier)

What is an Account?

An account is nothing but an outline of the transactions undertaken by the business in respect of persons, their representatives, and things.

For instance, when a business enters into transactions with suppliers or customers, both suppliers and customers act as separate accounts.

Similarly, businesses purchasing tangible items like plants, machinery, land, building etc treat each of the tangibles as individual accounts. Such accounts are related to things.

Thus, whenever a business undertakes transactions, it must identify the accounts involved and then apply the required accounting standards and golden accounting rules to record such transactions.

Types of Accounts

Accounts are classified into the following categories:

- Personal Account
- Natural Personal Account
- Artificial Personal Account
- Representative Personal Account
- Real Account
- Tangible Real Account
- Intangible Real Account
- Nominal Account

Further, an account is usually represented in a T-Format. Thus, a T Account has two sides to it. The left side is known as the debit side whereas the right side of an account is labeled as the credit side.

Books of Accounts for Service Business

For business or taxpayer engaged in the sale of services, it is required to maintain at least four which are the following:

General journal

General ledger

Cash receipt journal

Cash disbursement journal

Books of Accounts for Businesses Engaged in Sales of Goods or Properties

For business or taxpayer engaged in the sale of goods or properties, it is required to maintain at least six, which are the following:

General journal

General ledger

Cash receipt journal

Cash disbursement journal

Sales journal

Purchase journal

Trial Balance

Trial balance is a list of all the general ledger accounts (both revenue and capital) contained in the ledger of a business. This list will contain the name of each nominal ledger account and the value of that nominal ledger balance. Each nominal ledger account will hold either a debit balance or a credit balance.

The debit balance values will be listed in the debit column of the trial balance and the credit value balance will be listed in the credit column. The trading profit and loss statement and balance sheet and other financial reports can then be produced using the ledger accounts listed on the same balance.

Format of Trial Balance

TRIAL BALANCE

Accounting Capital Company
as on March, YYYY

Account	Debit	Credit
Purchases		
Sundry Debtors		
Stock (as on Apr, YYYY)		
Sales		
Cash at Bank		
Machinery		
Discount Received		
Bank Loan		
Bad Debts		
Sundry Creditors		
Carriage Outwards		
Capital		
Provision for Doubtful Debts		
Rent		
Discount Allowed		
TOTAL =		

Format of Trial Balance

Use of Trial Balance

It acts as a base to create the final accounts of a business such as an Income statement, a Trading A/C, and a Balance Sheet.

To prepare a trial balance it is important to ensure the arithmetic conceptual accuracy. Due to the dual aspect of accounting, the sum of total credits should be equal to the sum of total debits.

Due to its accuracy, tallied Trial Balances offer significant peace of mind regarding the accuracy of ledger balances.

It acts as a summarized form of all ledger balances, in case the debit and credit balances do not match then it is concluded that there is some error and the difference is temporarily transferred to a "Suspense A/C" and corrected afterward.

Auditors may decide to use it and transfer the account balances onto their auditing software. They can then perform various different kinds of inspections.

Financial Statements

Financial statements are written records that convey the business activities and the financial performance of a company. Financial statements are often audited by government agencies, accountants, firms, etc. to ensure accuracy and for tax, financing, or investing purposes.

Uses of Financial Statements

Following are some of the uses of financial statements:

1. **Determine the financial position of the business:** The most important use of financial statements is to provide information about the financial position of the business on a given date. This piece of information is used by various stakeholders in order to take important decisions regarding the business.
2. **To obtain credit**: Financial statements present the picture of the business to the potential lenders and this information can be used by them to provide additional credit for business expansion or restrict the credit so as to start recovery.
3. **Helps investors in decision making:** Financial statements contain all the essential information required by the potential investors for determining how much they want to invest in the business. It is also helpful in decision-making regarding the price per share that the investors want to invest. A sound financial statement is key to obtaining investments.
4. **Helps in policy-making:** The financial statements help the government in deciding the taxation and regulations policies based on the way the company is running its operations. The government bodies can tax a business based on the level of their income and assets.

5. **Useful for stock traders:** Financials statements help stock traders with the knowledge of the situation the company is in and therefore adjust their quotes accordingly.

Importance of Financial Statement

The significance of financial statements prevails in their service to persuade the diverse interests of distinct classes of parties such as creditors, public, management, etc.,

Importance to Management: Increase in size and intricacies of aspects influencing the business functions requires scientific and strategic access in the management of contemporary trading concerns. The management team needs up-to-date, precise, and methodical financial data for the intentions. Financial statements assist the management in comprehending the progress, prospects, and position of the business counterpart in the industry.

Importance to the Shareholders: Management is detached from control in the case of companies. Shareholders cannot take part in day-to-day business pursuits. However, the outcome of these pursuits should be disclosed to shareholders during the annual general body meeting in the form of financial statements.

Final Accounts

Final accounts give an idea about the profitability and financial position of a business to its management, owners, and other interested parties. All business transactions are first recorded in a journal. They are then transferred to a ledger and balanced. These final tallies are prepared for a specific period. The preparation of a final accounting is the last stage of the accounting cycle. It determines the financial position of the business. Under this, it is compulsory to make a trading account, the profit and loss account, and balance sheet.

The term "final accounts" includes the trading account, the profit and loss account, and the balance sheet.

Trading account

A trading account shows the results of the buying and selling of goods. This sheet is prepared to demonstrate the difference between the selling price and the cost price. The trading account is prepared to show the trading results of the business, e.g. gross profit earned or gross loss sustained by the business. It records the direct expenses of a business firm.

Profit and loss account

This account is prepared to ascertain the net profit/loss and expenses of a business during an accounting year. It records the indirect expenses of a business firm, like rent, salaries, and advertising expenses. Profit and loss a/c includes expenses and losses as well as income and gains, which have occurred in business other than the production of goods and services.

Balance sheet

The balance statement demonstrates the financial position of a business on a specific date. The financial position of a business is found by tabulating its assets and liabilities on a particular date. The excess of assets over liabilities represents the capital sunk into the business and reflects the financial soundness of a company.

Now it is known as the statement of financial position of the company.

CHAPTER V

Personnel Management

Introduction

Personnel management is the managerial function of estimating and classifying human resource requirements in order to achieve organisational goals through people at work and their interpersonal relationships.

Personnel management entails strategies for ensuring the right number of employees, the right mix of talent, training, and job performance.

According to Edwin B. Flippo – *"Personnel Management is the planning, organising, directing, and controlling of the procurement, development, compensation, integration and maintenance and separation of personnel to the end that individual, organisational and societal objectives are accomplished."*

"Personnel management is the administrative discipline of hiring and developing employees to increase their organisational value." Conducting job analyses, planning personnel needs and recruitment, selecting the right people for the right job, orienting and training, determining and managing wages and salaries, providing benefits and incentives, appraising performance, resolving disputes, and communicating with all employees at all levels are all part of this process."

Personnel department duties and responsibilities

Management of personnel refers to the business tasks dealing with people whether they are hired, paid or trained. But the word "management of human resources" replaces (or interchanges) the term "management of human resources."1 A company's human resources are its staff - its workers. Managing them nowadays, many organisations no longer have departments of personnel but have departments of human resources. Personnel, or human resources, the department is a department within an organization that is responsible for all employee services. This department's duties include attracting, maintaining and motivating employees while ensuring an organization's goals are met and values are upheld. A personnel department may include one or many employees depending on the size of the organization. The ultimate goal of all organizations is survival and growth. Various people at work do their best to achieve these organizational goals. But at some point, the organization is deprived of the help of some of its employees for various reasons such as death, retirement, dismissal, disability, benefits, etc.

A personnel department, also known as a human resources department, is one of the departments within an organisation that is in charge of all employee services. The responsibilities of this department include attracting, retaining, and motivating employees while ensuring that the organization's goals and values are met. Depending on the size of the company, a personnel department may have one or many employees.

The personnel department of a company handles a variety of critical functions that help meet the needs of the company's owners, managers, and employees. Employees are hired and trained, company policies and procedures are implemented, specific performance issues are handled, employee salaries are determined, fair labour laws are followed, employees are terminated, and so on.

Recruiting, hiring, and training new employees are three of the most important functions of a personnel department. Personnel department employees must post new job openings as they become available, interview qualified candidates, and hire the best candidates for the job. When new employees are hired, they must fill out payroll forms, healthcare packages, benefit packages, and other paperwork, all of which is kept on file in the personnel department.

Employee relations are also handled by personnel departments. When there are misunderstandings or disagreements between management and employees, personnel department employees are frequently called upon to mediate the situation. They accept written complaints about employees, investigate them, and decide what action to take.

Moreover, the company needs more employees as it expands. The objective of the department of work is to help the company acquire, develop and retain the appropriate employees.

Personnel duties

1.Organizational policies Department

The achievement of the objectives of an organization and the upholding of values includes the development of organizational policies. Personnel collaborates with senior managers to develop and implement policies for all staff within the organization. The personnel departments codify these policies and deliver them to workers, which are frequently referred to as an employee manual.

This information is used for a variety of reasons such as payroll, and local, state, and federal employment laws.

This data is utilised for a range of reasons, including payroll, municipal, state, and federal workers' legislation.

2. Relations with staff

The staff department creates and administers employee initiatives with managers and guarantees fair treatment for workers. It comprises the collection of information on elements impacting the company's commitment in order to discover strategies of improving the morality and retention of employees.

3. Employee Information

A department of personnel organizes, manages, and secures the organization's documents and data for each employee. These covers pay, perks, assessments of performance and other documentation. Documents and registrations are generally saved in files, as are a secured human resources database.

4. Selection and recruitment

Workers recruit and choose employees, if necessary, alongside supervisors and senior managers. When positions are provided, the staff department offers job vacancies, recruits applicants and interviews with management and managers to choose workers who match the criteria and objectives of the business.

What are the HR or Personnel department's responsibilities and functions?

Consequently, the number of responsibilities is almost limitless, so we can conclude that HR functions are vast and diversified.

When building the staff or personnel department and developing a strategy plan, all these functions must be defined. Let's have a peek at each other.

1. Staff management

Managing staff administratively is one of the key duties in the staff department These include contract management, payments, permits, sick leave, yearly leave, maternity/paternity absences, etc. This is entirely administrative, time-consuming job and needs strong coordination of teams with the entire team, staff and authorities in order to be able to prevent future mistakes and difficulties. To carry perform these responsibilities, many human resources departments utilize Excel Tablets. However, in these days, human resources management software allows you to automate most of this labor and to save 40 percent of your time.

2. Employment and selection of employees

The HR Department also mainly attracts and selects the top personnel.

First of all, the team must focus on its employer branding to interest the most demanded professionals in the field. For example, Google has become, thanks to its outstanding reputation as an employer, one of the most popular corporations in the world. A research by LinkedIn has shown that 75% of professionals who are engaged in searching for jobs evaluate the image of an enterprise before requesting a job. And 96 percent think their reputation has a favorable impact on their income.

The following stage is the selection procedure for the interview, the identification and selection of the most suitable and possible qualified individuals, after professionals apply. This process is organized by recruiting software, which enhances applicant experience, and provides reports and analysis with a single click.

3. Management of compensation and incentive

Employee wages and perks are also accountable for human resources. This involves the determination of an adequate salary rate for each position, taking consideration of the value it brings to the firm, the salary on the labor market and its parameters. This involves frequent pay assessments by employees, arranging incentives with providers, such as restaurant and medical insurance tickets, defining goals and giving performing benefits.

Ensuring and satisfying wage expectations of employees is a major element of this duty to promote employee motivation and well-being.

4. Positive Work Climate Devolution

The working environment at this firm is one of the major elements since it has a vital impact on the welfare and productivity of personnel. Experts agree that the working environment is positive:

- Improve productivity
- Lower absenteeism.
- Enhances engagement or motivation.

How can the staff determine if the business has a pleasant working environment? Workplace climate surveys are the most popular tools because they contribute to the collection of important information on staff satisfaction, the recognition of problems and improvement in decision-making. They may be automated and sent, so that staff can react more easily. It is extremely simple to promote a good working environment. Space has a substantial impact, for example. Various studies have shown the productivity of an open workplace design to rise by 20% and natural light to 40%.

Moreover, the working conditions were one of the highest values of 22% of Best Workplaces employees.

5. Evaluation Employee Performance

Another human resource management function is the evaluation of employee performance. The performance and dedication of each employee to the firm should be reviewed periodically. For each member of the organization, specific and quantifiable objectives are important and the assessment system is developed beforehand.

Using employee performance evaluation software is commonly done. The use of a cloud-based platform gives multiple individuals the opportunity to evaluate an employee, which allows them to acquire more information. This allows both qualitative and quantitative evaluation of human resources.

6. Staff Service and Training Pragrammes

The staff department should also establish training programmes to guarantee that every worker in the business is grown and that vital skills are developed for the future of the firm. This is not just a technique to recruit and retain people, but also to maximize your human capital's potential. Courses, training, career development and internal advancement are essential human resources duties.

Ideally, a plan should be outlined in the department:

The company's present and future demands.

A differentiated job-related training strategy.

Plan of implementation via courses, workshops for conferences.

7. Relationships Laboratory

Human resources also address labor issues and negotiate with syndical representatives (where they exist). Including:

- Conversation between employers and staff.
- In the case of internal disagreement, mediate amongst workers.
- Negotiate with unions or stakeholders' employee rights.
- Act as the spokesperson of the firm or employee if appropriate

Ultimately, any corporate conflicts, recruiting, salary rules, etc., should be addressed by the department.

8. Health and Safety

In developing and implementing occupational safety and health regulations, HR plays an essential role. In several areas, this may be a very difficult responsibility, because we deal with employee health and safety. The crew has to:

- When rules change, implement safety precautions.
- Ensure compliance with rules
- Negotiate trade union and employee safety measures.

Planning of workforce

What is the planning of manpower?

Manpower planning is the method through which the ideal number of workers to complete a project, work or objective may be estimated in due course. Capacity planning covers criteria such as a number of staff, various skill kinds, time duration, etc. It is an unending process to ensure that the enterprise has the optimal resources available, taking into account future initiatives and the replacement of the executive staff as necessary. It is sometimes termed the planning of human resources.

Large companies typically focus on pipeline forecasts and future prospects. If these possibilities become true business, they will need to work on them. But the issue is that when they recruited many individuals to work on a nearly safe project, the project didn't begin in time at the last minute. What would the firm do with the extra trained workforce? The other issue is that if you wait for a project till the last moment, then when the project starts, you may not have enough work. The workforce planning method resolves these issues.

Importance of workforce management

1. Management Key: Four managerial functions are dependent on manpower, i.e. planning, organization, management and controlling. All these managerial operations are aided by human resources. Staffing, therefore, becomes a cornerstone to all management tasks.

2. Efficient use - An essential role in today's industrialization is becoming efficient management of employees. The establishment of huge companies requires large-scale personnel management. It may be performed successfully by means of personnel.

1. Motivation- The staffing role includes not only placing the proper personnel into good work but also motivating programs, i.e. incentives to develop incentives for continued employer engagement and employment in an enterprise. All sorts of incentive schemes therefore become an important element of the personnel role.

2. Better human relations- If human relationships grow and are solid, a concern can sustain itself. Human interactions are strengthened via effective control, clear communication, effective monitoring and leadership. The employee role also ensures workforce education and development leading to cooperation and a stronger relationship with the human being.

3. Higher productivity- The level of productivity improves if resources are used as effectively as feasible. The minimal loss of time, money, effort and energy will result in greater output. The workforce and related activities make this feasible (Performance appraisal, training and development, remuneration).

Need to plan workforce

Manpower planning is a two-phased procedure, as staff planning analyses not only existing human resources but also produces workforce projections and draws jobs. The company benefits from manpower planning in the following ways:

1. Shortages and surpluses can be recognized to allow for rapid response when necessary.

2. workforce planning is a basis for all recruiting and selection initiatives.

3. It also contributes to reducing labor costs by identifying the extra workforce and avoiding excess employment.

4. It also contributes to identifying the skills available in an enterprise and training programmes may thus be developed.

5. It contributes to corporate development and diversity. Human resources may be easily accessible and utilized in the best possible way through employee planning.

6.It allows the organization to understand how important the management of human resources eventually contributes to the stability of a company.

Employment Sources

Employee recruiting sources (with their pros and disadvantages): internal and external sources!

The most essential part of the recruiting process is the search and communication of potential applicants on the company openings.

The candidates might be accessible inside the organization or outside. There are basically two recruitment sources, internally and outside.

(A) Internal Sources: The organization has the best personnel... When a vacancy occurs, an employee who is on the payroll may be assigned a vacancy. Internal sources include promotion, transfer and demotion in some circumstances. In the case of a higher position, all other staff of the organization are motivated to work hard. Internal advertising can alert staff about such a position.

Internal Sources Methods:

1. Transfers: Transfer entail moving people from existing positions to similar positions. There are no changes in status, accountability or prestige. With transfers, the number of people does not grow.

2. Promotions: promotions refer to the transfer of people to jobs with more status and more salary. Promotions: The higher roles that are empty within the organization can be filled. The number of people in the organization is not increased by a promotion.

A person who becomes higher will quit his current post. Promotion will encourage employees to enhance their performance to promote them as well.

3. Current staff: The current staff are notified about probable vacancies. The personnel are thoroughly aware of their relationships with people. Management is freed of prospective applicants.

The people selected by the staff can typically be adequate for the work since they know the needs of different roles. The present workers are fully accountable for the proposed personnel and guarantee their good conduct and performance.

(B) External Sources : If current personnel are not suitable, all organizations must seek external sources for higher-level recruiting. When expansions take place, more people are needed.

Below are the external sources:

External Sources Methods:

1. Publicity: a recruitment strategy commonly employed by qualified workers, clerics and senior employees. Publicity may be offered through professional journals and newspapers. This publicity attracts a huge number of applications with extremely varied quality.

It is a specific responsibility to prepare good advertising. If a firm wishes to dissimulate its name, the candidates may be asked to apply to Post Bag or Box Number or any advertising agency for a "blind advertisement.

2. Employment exchanges: the government operates employment exchanges in India. It is commonly used as a source of recruiting for unqualified, semi-qualified, qualified, clerical jobs etc. In some circumstances, company organizations were required compulsory to inform the exchange of their openings. In the past these agencies were only employed as a last resort by companies. Employment seekers and employees will be contacted by the trade.

3. Schools, colleges, and universities: The direct recruitment of specific employment (i.e. placement) requiring technical or professional qualifications from educational institutions is becoming a regular practice. A tight relationship between businesses and schools helps to acquire qualified applicants. During their studies, the pupils are seen. This allows the recruitment of junior managers or management trainees.

4. Existing Employee Recommendation: The existing workers are familiar with the firm as well as the candidate. Some firms, therefore, urge their existing staff to help them acquire applications from people they are familiar with.

In some circumstances, compensation may also be granted if the applicants who are recommended are actually chosen by the firm. The morale of employees will be damaged if suggestion leads to favoritism.

5. Gates Plant: Some workers appear at the gate of the factory on a daily basis. For unqualified or semi-skilled work, this recruiting strategy is particularly common in India. The desirable candidates are chosen by the supervisors of the first line. The primary drawback of the method is that it is not possible for the individual chosen to be able to work.

6. Casual Callers: The vacant post may be also used by employees who come to the firm for work informally. It is the cheapest recruitment strategy. This recruitment strategy is highly common in sophisticated nations.

7. Centrally applied file: a file may be retained for previous applicants not picked previously. Apps in the files should be verified at regular periods in order to maintain the file active.

8. Labor syndicates: All recruits generally originate from trade unions in specific areas like as construction, hotels, seafarers, etc. Managementally, it is favorable since it reduces recruitment expenditures. In other industries, however, unions might be requested either as goodwill gestures or as politeness for the union to propose candidates.

9. Labor entrepreneurs: The recruitment of trained and semi-skilled laborer's in the brick clinical business is still common in India. The contractors remain in contact with the workforce and bring the employees where necessary. They receive fees for the amount of people they provide.

10. Former workers: In the case of laying off or having left the plant alone, employees can be taken back if they choose to join the company (provided their record is good).

11. Additional Sources: In addition to these important sources of external recruiting, a number of other sources are used from time to time by firms. These include special lectures given by recruits in various universities, however, these talks seem to be not directly concerned with recruiting.

There are then video films that are distributed in order to exhibit the history and development of the firm to diverse concerns and institutions. These videos introduce different audiences to the history of the firm, which creates interest in them.

Different companies organize trade exhibitions that attract numerous forward-looking workers. A specific working group (say married females) who worked before their marriage might often be advertised.

These females can also demonstrate that they are a very good supply of labor. Similarly, the physically disabled labor market exists. Finding fresh recruitment sources also helps visits to other firms.

The adaptiveness of external recruitment resources:

external recruitment sources are appropriate for the following reasons:

(i) the characteristics necessary, including the will, skill, ability, know-how etc., can be found from outside sources.

(ii) it can aid the organization's development of new ideas, improved approaches and enhanced processes.

(iii) Candidate selection shall be conducted without prior thought or reservation.

(iv) The employee cost will be minimum because of the minimum scale of pay for applicants chosen under that technique.

(v) In the human resources mix it will be helpful to enter new people with diverse experiences and talents.

(vi) Current staff will also extend their personalities.

(vii) Entries from outside of qualitative will be in the organization's long-term benefit.

WORKERS and SUPERVISORS trains and unveils.

To make a firm prosper, it must handle risk correctly. One approach to assist this objective is to provide highly effective training.

The organization will be much more efficient with options such as leadership training seminars and supervisory development programs, as, among many other things, it will help meet regulatory obligations.

You prevent audits, penalties, legal proceedings when you invested in managers' coaching, leadership training, or any other kind of managers' training.

Training Benefits

The supervisors will utilize development programmes to cope effectively with job tasks. Zoe Training gives a full list for a more detailed look at the top professional development subjects. Some of the advantages are:

To develop skills and know-how, which will enhance the dynamism and productivity of the job, in an efficient and effective fashion.

Learn how to operate in order to prevent proceedings, accidents and penalties.

Develop collaboration, communication and many other competencies that will improve the company's internal operations.

Special roles and managers in transportation

For an enterprise, supervisors and managers are quite crucial. They are the organization's front line and their involvement throughout training is crucial. The supervisors always have to:

Understand the legal requirements of the training.

Follow correct legal processes in order to allow workers to follow them.

be at ease with the organizational policies used and the laws affecting employment.

Acknowledge the relevant and irrelevant legislation as well.

Identify training essential to enhance the quality of your job for workers.

Understand the value of training for the development and motivation of workers' abilities.

Understand the link between training and productivity/growth of companies.

Know the resources for certain personnel accessible.

Guaranteeing courteous and equitable treatment for persons employed in the firm at all times. – – bis Remain dedicated to safeguarding the rights of employer and employee alike.

The supervisor is essentially an employer's representative in any firm. All rights must be properly understood to ensure that breaches are prevented. Then you need to know how to handle complaints and concerns.

It is the great obligation of supervisors to ensure that any issues arising before a lawsuit arises or an employee just stops. The role also involves getting people comfortable with duties and tasks.

When a complaint is lodged or legal actions are taken by an employee, the legal parties concerned examine the efforts made to comply with all applicable legislation. If a tribunal investigates reprisals, discrimination and other claims and finds that company rules have not been effectively applied and disseminated, significant difficulties will arise. A supervisor will need continuing training to build the skills, trust and knowledge required to deal with all human resources concerns on a daily basis.

Workers

Training and development of workers refers to a company's ongoing attempts to increase its employees' performance.

Companies are aimed at training and development of employees by employing a wide variety of educational tools in recent years.

Investing in training and development for employees is not only a motivator for more business owners; it can also help the organization generate highly competent employees. The importance of training and development for employees is explained in this article. It also highlights the many techniques that companies utilize to teach their staff.

Employee Development And Breaking Down

Although the phrases "training" and "development" are used interchangeably, the two ideas nevertheless differ somewhat. The distinctions pertain to the application scope. In essence, a training programme, such as learning how to do a certain process with precision or how to use a piece of machine, provides very precise and quantifiable goals.

Instead, a development programme aims to acquire more competencies that may be utilized in a variety of circumstances. Skills include decision-making, communication and leadership.

Employee development and training benefits

While investment in staff training has certain disadvantages, the advantages of such programmes significantly exceed them. The advantages are:

1. Additional weeks

If a firm owner attentively examines his employee, two or more of his employees are likely to lack specific qualifications. A training programme offers the chance to introduce the necessary skills to staff. Likewise, a development programme supports the expansion of all employees' knowledge base.

This enables the owners of companies to overcome any deficiencies and weak connections within their businesses. Each employee will therefore be able to fulfil his or her duty and deal efficiently with any assignment.

2. Employee's improved performance

An employee trained from time to time is better able to increase his productivity of his or her task. Every employee is well-known through training programmes with safety measures and appropriate procedures when doing fundamental duties. A training programme also helps to develop a trust in employees, because the industry and the obligations of their job will be better understood.

3. Boosts company profile and Reputation

As said before, training for staff is not only beneficial for the staff, but also for the company. Frequent training and development programmes are one approach to promote the company's employer brand, therefore ensuring that the top employees in competing companies and graduates take pride in this. A firm training its staff will make potential new workers more attractive, especially those seeking to enhance their qualifications.

4. Innovation

It promotes innovation when staff are continuously trained and upgraded. The training programmes, when faced with problems at work, allow people to be more autonomous and innovative.

Common employee training and development training methods

While new training strategies emerge every day, a few of conventional training methodologies have been extremely successful. Including:

1. Orientation

Guidance training is critical to new recruits' performance. It matters not if a manual, a one-on-one session or a lecture is used for the instruction. It is important to provide new workers with information about the background, strategy, task, vision and objectives of the company. This training provides new staff the chance to learn about corporate policies, laws and regulations.

2. Lectures.

Lectures are very effective when the goal is to supply a big group with the same material at once. In this way, no individual training is needed and hence cost savings are achieved. Readings also provide certain drawbacks, though. For one thing, they focus on one-way communication, leaving little possibility for criticism. The trainer may also find it difficult to evaluate the degree of material knowledge in a large group.

3. Computer Based Training (CBT)

This technique is the main mode of communication between the trainer and staff, using computers and computer-based tutorials. The programmes are intended to deliver educational information and facilitate the learning process.

The primary advantage of computerized training (cbt) is the ability to study at the most convenient period at each employee's own speed. It also helps decrease the overall cost of training for its personnel for a business. By lowering the training time, minimizing teacher demand and reducing travel costs, costs are decreased.

For any organisation today, knowledge and skills are important. Based on its physical structure and intellectual capital, companies are rated. Regular training and development programmes are the easiest approach to building and strengthening an intellectual capital company. The organisation also costs more than if it employed well-trained people to help unskilled staff. Other benefits of training and development include enhancing employee performance, increasing the reputation of the business and tackling weak linkages within the corporation.

What is the promotion?

Promotion?

Promotion is a rising movement of employees to another job in the company, which is more active within the organisation. The new position will affect the employee's income, state, responsibilities and grade of employment or appointment. In general the company sees the vacancy value of employees more than the current position of the employee. Unlike promotion, which increases an employee's pay without a commensurate change in employment status, it is known as a 'upgrade.' But if promotion does not affect wages, it is known as 'dry promotion.' Promotion is an internal movement technique.

Promotion Types

Promotion for personnel in an organisation may be divided into three different types:

- **Horizontal promotion:** when an employee has been moved to the same category, the promotion is called horizontal. An example is a junior staff member promoted to senior staff. The promotion might happen when an individual moves from department to department and plant to plant within the same department.

- **vertical promotion:** this is promoted in a way that involves a rise in compensation, prestige, power and responsibility from the lower category to the lower category. Promotion usually denotes 'vertical advancement.'
- **Dry promotion:** it is called 'dry promotion' when promotion without wage increases. For example, a lesser level director gets promoted without an increase in income or compensation to a senior level manager. Either the resource/fund crisis is promoted in the organisation or workers strive for status or power rather than money.

The aims of promotion are as follows:

1. To identify and use an employee's expertise and knowledge to enhance organisational efficiency.
2. To reward and promote greater productivity for staff.
3. Enhancing the competitive spirit and encouraging staff to gain skills, information and so on.
4. Promoting and boosting employee satisfaction.
5. Building loyalty to the organisation between employees.
6. Promoting excellent ties with others.
7. Enhance the sense of affiliation.
8. To retain talented and skilled individuals.
9. Trained, skilled and hard-workers attraction.
10. To impress the other staff that, if they work well, they too have chances.

Advantages of promotion

- The current employees know the norms, processes and culture of the company, and do not need an inductive programme, because workers are aware of the way the organisation works.
- The firm has vast information and knowledge about employees of the past.
- It might boost the morale of the workforce to provide internal staff with opportunities.
- A favorable image is created in the organisation

Disadvantages of promotion

- Published work may need abilities not currently available inside the company
- Promoting a person in the organisation might lead to resentment among other workers who feel they deserve the job instead of the individual

promoted.

• The number of candidates to choose from may be either high or too restricted.

• It is possible to promote less skilled personnel than those from outside the organisation in accordance with internal recruitment standards or the Employment Equity Act. Most home candidates stalled for such a lengthy time and would not favorably give fresh suggestions.

Retirement

Remission means leaving a career or a job or an active life. An individual might also withdraw by reducing employment or working hours. Many people decide to retire when they are aged or unable to do their job. People can also retire if they have the right to private and government pension benefits, while some are forced to retire if a person is no longer permitted to work under physical conditions (by disease or accident). Most industrialized countries have pension plans for old age pensions, either by employers or the governments. In many cultures, pension retirement is considered a workers' right now; it has been a long battle whether it is right, intellectual, social, cultural and political. In many western nations it is a right included in the national constitutions.

This last retirement point is being deferred more by choosing to remain in the expanding state of countries before retirement

In order to enable or encourage private-sector retirement, it has implemented a wide array of laws. In age discrimination under the Employment Act of 1967 (ADEA) the maximum pension age requirements and obligatory payments until age 70 were legally limited. Both practises have been abolished since that time. Other law has banned pension plans from stopping pension accumulation at the age of 65 or restricting old new workers' eligibility to enter into corporate pensions. Retreats take place toward the end of their working life. An employee has another overannuation age. Removal will vary from retirement. If the employee overrides and leaves the enterprise, he or she will have several advantages. A privilege is denied to the employee who leaves.

Secondly, retirement occurs at the end of the working life of an individual, but can occur at any time.

Thirdly, the surrender does not remove any distressing connection from the retiring individual, but its lack is likely to make the employer feel awful.

VOLUNTARY RETIREMENT SCHEME (VRS)

Beginning in the 1980s, for valid reasons, the commercial, as well as public sectors, have transferred their surplus work to their homes not through cutbacks, sino by a new programme called the VRS voluntary pension plan. The VRS employees‘ withdrawal pay is regarded as a poor approach to reduce personnel strength and save time. Several companies, including Hindustan Lever, Siemens and TISCO, managed the strategy well and succeeded quite well. TISCO assigned Rs.100 crore for its VRS in 1997. Within five years, the company opted to reduce its staff by 68,000 to 55,000 and was reacted positively.

Various Methods Of Testing, Retrenchment

What is Retrenchment?

Removal is a disagreeable part of contemporary business and everyday life. In order to fulfill or meet operational objectives, an enterprise or organisation find that it needs to decrease the number of personnel, the fundamental concept is the reduction.

Good and Bad Side Of Retrenchment

- The beautiful aspect of rediscovery is that it provides firms and staff an excellent chance to join the organisation. The company decreases its number of employees and leaves people on redundancies. For the employees who had been for a long period with the company, that would be large money. They are happy to go and the start interview is typically an enjoyable opportunity. I say "generally" because some folks think it's time to vent their company grievances.|
- Often the unpleasant side of the removal are those folks unwilling to go for work! Despite all HR training, these exit interviews are the hardest. And I'm not afraid to confess it breaks my heart! At that time, it becomes a moot point whether or not these people should have been limited. And all the sensations "why me" come out! They've got no replies!

Selecting Employee for Retrenchment

The employees are selected for several reasons. Employees are frequently chosen based on job term, potential or corporate success. The company's service length refers to the term "last in, first out" in general (LIFO). The technique of LIFO retrenchment is meant to protect long-term LIFO workers. This might seem fair to the individual who has been working for a longer time but it may not be in the best interests of the firm. Another way is to create opportunities first and foremost by removing older personnel. This might be problematic since the level of knowledge could be reduced and loyalty to the company could be eroded. On the basis of their performance, employees may also be picked. Initially, this method is to eliminate low-performing staff. This depends partly on the performance evaluation mechanism of the company. In order to ensure fairness, organizations using this approach must provide employees feedback and improvements. The strategy used by companies is to assess the potential for future workers and first of all reduce the potential of employees. This approach is based on assessments of performance and procedural equity similar to performance. Removals may also be done freely, giving employees who desire to be redundant the opportunity. Employment freedom can also occur if employees are offered financial incentives to leave work. This method of layoff management encourages workers' redundancy. However, this might lead to the departure of great workers (persons the firm wishes to maintain).

Types of Retrenchment Strategy

There are 10 types of Retrenchment strategies:

1. Turnaround

The phrase "turnaround" refers to ways of changing adverse patterns in the performance measurements of the firm. This covers management actions to reverse falling trends in performance metrics such as diminishing market share, decreasing sales, lower profitability, increased expenses, deteriorating debt-equity ratios, inadequate cash flow, serious issues with working capital, etc. They mean managerial actions that turn the healthy business around. The strategies utilised to emerge from the crisis varied instance after instance and company after company. The turnaround strategy often emphasises improved internal efficiency, and any actions or combinations that follow can lead to a company being unsuccessful.

2. Divorce Strategy

The company that has bought assets and divisions will assess in divestments if assets or divisions are available in the global corporate plan to maximise value. Such assets or splits will be increased when they do not meet the objective.

The sale of a piece or part of a corporation is known as "dislodging." It is generally used to accumulate cash to buy or invest more strategically. It also employs unproductive commercial entities.

3. Strategy for settlement

A firm might decline if losses persist over several years. Previous profits (reserves) compensate for losses, but the circumstance is clearly not continued for too much.

The owner may decide to wind up the company to avoid further exacerbation of losses in case of technological obsoleteness, absence of a market for the company's goods, losses in cash, deficit in the management of funds and lack of management ability. For a strategic purpose, a business unit might also be liquidated. In the case that the firm does not consider the company attractive to restart the company, this strategic alternative is used. The selling of the whole company is a winding-up. For the physical worth, all of a company's assets in parts are known as "liquidation." Any liquidation is preferable than bankruptcy for the interests of the owner.

4. Captive company strategy

A company is termed 'captive company,' which is reduced by the vertical reverse integration. In exchange for ensuring that the other business acquires a certain quantity of the captive's product, one enterprise is imprisoned by another corporation.

5. Harvest Strategy

The firm uses the present company in this way completely without further costs. It is a strategy of reduction in assets that control or decreases an undertaking's investment and extracts the greatest possible investment. The business exits the industry when it obtains the highest possible returns.

The company pauses new capital investments, advertising, R&D and so on, to maximise the unit's short- to medium-long cash flow before liquidation. The company resorts to this technique when product/market segments exhibit poor, declining but nonetheless good profitability. The firm intends to reduce its market share by giving the company the highest short-term profit, ultimately withdrawal from the market. This approach can be utilised for collecting cash for other lucrative ventures.

6. Transformation strategy

When a corporation significantly changes its beliefs and operations, usually from one company to the next. In general, strategic adjustments are quite important. The whole organisation needs much flexibility. Such a plan is tough to adopt.

7. Leadership Strategy.

The goal of this method is to get a business in the lead so that the declining market is primarily for itself. Enterprises in failing industries use this strategy as a dominating player in the field to stay far away from all other companies in the industry. The strategy asks for the so-called "exit obstacles" to be reduced and rivals excluded.

The firm may help its competitors often overcome their exit barriers and therefore ensure that they are the survivor. The leader communicated to other rivals, by adopting an aggressive price and marketing campaign, that he will not give up without battling, which will raise prices for everyone involved.

The business stresses its commitment to remain in the industry. The company is designed to be a market leader in the shrinking market and hence create superior industrial returns.

8. Niche Strategy

'Niche' means concentrating on a product and a market.

It reflects the regular activities of small businesses in a relatively low-risk way.

Generally speaking, such organisations, which might lead to legal, labour and management challenges, are hesitant to expand. They are thus pleased with their existing position and would want to draw on top local knowledge and select a relatively narrow market area.

Niche marketing means the financing, maintenance and development of unique products and services for profitable segments of the market. For large firms, these niches are too small due to the lack of economy of scale. A niche market may be seen as a well-defined range of prospective consumers which are not addressed by the primary providers. Typically, a specialised dealer uses the loyalty business approach to maintain a good sales volume. The niche method consists of the discovery of profitable niches which dominate the niches of the defeated industry.

Attractive niches or niches that have severe inelastic needs are either not falling. Typically, the low demand levels of these remaining markets cannot help more than one firm so that not all rivals may regard it as a solution.

9. Failure Strategy

When you hear the phrase bankruptcy, people initially think about dread and sadness. Though after bankruptcy there will be a time of adjustment, it must not be associated with fear. In certain cases, insolvency registration might just as readily be viewed as a route to a new start. Most of us live with debts, be they mortgages, auto payments, student loans or credit cards. For many reasons, debts, including loss of jobs, divorce or medical disability, might become unsustainable. Strategically, bankruptcy can provide you and your family with a way to remove and begin their responsibilities.

10. Policies for the end of the game.

The final strategy or decreasing industry strategy is a framework to analyse and develop solutions that are appropriate to the firm in a particular environment and the nature and causes behind declines.

While the PRODUCT LIFE CYCLe sector has reached the declining stage of the decrease, generally it has falling demand and overcapacity problems, it may still provide companies with COMPETITIVE ADVANTAGES an attractive return over competing suppliers. For some, leaving the industry directly rather than staying on might be acceptable. the market structure, the characteristics and factors that influence competitiveness in relation to the level of the MARKET CONCENTRATION, the perception of the factors by the company itself, the reasons for the decline, the rate with which the demand declines and the involvement of market segments;

Industrial fatigue, discipline Industrial relations, industrial relations: industrial relations: industrial relations:

"Industry" covers "Industry" and "Connections." Any productive action involving a human is referred to by industry

(a) primary activities, such as farming, fishing, forestry, forestry, horticulture, mining etc.

(b) secondary businesses, such as manufacturing, construction, trade, transport, trade, banking etc.

Based on their combined attitudes and managerial practices, the links between industry and workforce, in particular, may be described as relationships and interactions in the industry; they are designed not only to strengthen management and employees but also industry and the economy in general.

Industrial discipline: industrial discipline implies the orderly functioning of workers of an industrial firm, in accordance with fixed standards, regulations and conventions. Discipline is a force that motivates a person, in order to attain an objective, to respect standards, regulations and processes.

Industrial Relations

The term 'Industrial Relations' comprises 'Industry' and 'relations'. Industry means any productive activity in which an individual is engaged. It includes- (a) primary activities like agriculture, fisheries, plantation, forestry, horticulture, mining etc. etc. and (b) Secondary activities like manufacturing, construction, trade, transport, commerce, banking, communication etc.

Industrial relations may be defined as the relations and interactions in the industry particularly between the labour and management as a result of their composite attitudes and approaches in regard to the management of the affairs of the industry, for the betterment of not only the management and the workers but also of the industry and the economy as a whole.

Industrial Relations – Importance of IR

1. The labours today are more educated and they are aware of their responsibilities and rights. Management has to deal with them not merely as factors of production, but as individuals having human dignity and self-respect. The objective is to change the traditional views of management and labour towards each other and develop mutual understanding and co-operation and work towards the achievement of a common goal. Good industrial relations lead to industrial peace and an increase in production.

2. Joint consultation between employees and management paves the way for industrial democracy and contribute to the growth of the organisation.

3. Conducive industrial relations motivate the workers to give increased output. Problems are solved through mutual discussions, workers' participation, suggestion schemes, joint meeting, etc. Good industrial relations, increase labour efficiency and productivity.

4. With increased productivity, the management is in a position to offer financial and non-financial incentives to workers

The fundamental prerequisites for a successful program in industrial relations are:

1. **Top management support:** - Since industrial relations are a functional personnel department, its authority must be derived from the company. This will be secured by ensuring that the director of industrial relations reports to the President, chairman or vice-president of an organisation from a leading authority.

2. **Sound Personnel Policies:** – This constitutes an organization's business philosophy and guides it in reaching its judgments on human relations. 1. The aim of these policies is to decide what to do about the many problems that occur daily during the operation of the organisation before an emergency develops. Policies can only succeed if they are implemented from above to below at all levels of a company.

3. **Professionals should establish appropriate practices:** – to support the implementation of an organization's policies. If the purpose is adequately converted into action, a set of processes is necessary.The Industrial Relations Department rules and practices are a "management

tool" that allows a supervisor to take the timekeeper, rate adjustor, complaint reporter and merit rater ahead of his or her work.

4. Detailed supervision training: - In order to ensure appropriate application and implementation of organisational policies and practices by workers in industrial relations, job supervisors should be extensively taught in order to communicate their relevance to employees. In addition, they should be taught in management and communication.

5. Results monitoring: A continuing assessment of the Industrial Relations Program is important in order to correctly analyse existing practices and to monitor, if they present themselves, certain unwanted trends. Continuous research should complement the follow-up to work turnover, absenteeism, the morality of government, grievances and suggestions for employees, etc. in order to guarantee the best possible adaptation to corporate demands and employee satisfaction with policies. The following should be done. In exit interviews, trade union demands and management meetings and formal social sciences research, indications of the areas of concern are identified.

Main Aspects of IR

(1)Promoting and developing good labour management relations,

(2) preserving industrial peace and preventing industrial conflict; and

(3) developing industrial democracy.

The scope of business interactions includes:

(a) employee, employee and superior relationships or managers relationships.

(b) Collective trade union-management relations. It is termed relationships between union and management.

(c) Trade unions, employers' organisations and the government in their collective interactions.

Scott, Clothier and Spiegel pointed out that business connections must achieve the highest possible individual growth and desirable working relations amongst individuals

The industrial relations objectives are set forth below:

(i) Ensure a high degree of mutual understanding and goodwill across all the industries involved in the production process to ensure the interests of work and management.

(ii) to improve productivity by stopping greater labour sales and frequent absence.

(iii) Preventing industrial disputes and developing amicable labor-management relations for a country's industrial development.

(iv) Establishing and maintaining Industrial Democracy on the basis of labour partnership, in order that individual personalities are completely acknowledged and become civilised citizens of the country, by sharing the organisational benefits, but also by associating labour in the decision-making process.

(v) Bridging government control over loss-making enterprises or regulating production for the public interest.

(vi) To reduce strikes, lockouts, gheraos and other pressures by giving the workers with higher salaries, better conditions of work and limited benefits.

(vii) The need to re-shape complex social relations, adaptable to technologic progress, by controlling and disciplining their members, and by adjusting their conflicting interests, by bridging a gap between the imbalanced, disordered and unfair social order (which has been the result of industrial development) and the need.

Industry discipline

Industrial discipline refers to the orderly working of the employees of an industrial undertaking in accordance with established rules, regulations and conventions. Discipline is a force that prompts an individual to observe rules, regulations and procedures to attain an objective

Industrial Discipline Importance: Discipline plays a key function in the company in maintaining industrial harmony and increasing production. Management is responsible for framing the rules and regulations of organisations in line with the country's existing labour legislation.

What is required?

The effective work relations plan, which is affected by three major aspects, represents the personnel's point of view:

- Personal thinking
- Awareness of policy and anticipated social response

industrial discipline principles are set forth below for ensuring a good disciplinary system:

Principles

1. **Knowledge of the Rules:** workers (the supervisor and the employee) must be fully aware of what excellent conduct is and what incentives may arise. To this end, in cooperation with the employees, the organisation should create a Code of Discipline.

The rules, regulatory provisions and processes considered necessary to preserve discipline should be contained in writing in this code. All those responsible and the penalties for their infringements must be disclosed. Code of discipline in an employee's manual should be published.

2. Prompt action: Inquire into any breaches and infringements swiftly. The offender links the punishment with the act he committed if the penalty is applied soon following the misbehavior.

The subordinate therefore try in the future to prevent the infringement. The following principle is "strike the iron when it's hot." The longer the wait, the more forgetful you are and the more punishments you believe are unworthy.

3. Fair action: all actions of discipline should be consistently and consistently punished. For the same offense, everyone should receive the same punishment.

If various regulations apply to individuals, management is accused of favoritism. An action to be fair has to be characterised by the following:

(a) Any infringements, large or little, shall be properly punished.

(a) For equal indiscipline all persons should get equal punishment.

(c) Incompatible managerial behaviour leads to doubt in subordinates' thinking.

Discipline should always be consistently applied.

(d) a thorough inquiry into the alleged infringement.

(f) An chance to explain its conduct should always be given to the employee.

(f) Management always has the burden of demonstrating the infringement.

4. Well-defined procedure: explicitly lay forth the method for disciplinary action. Appeal and examination of all disciplinary proceedings should be allowed for under definite and clear rules. The following steps should be included:

(a) The supervisor shall be assured that there has been some breach of the regulations.

(b) The supervisor shall indicate the nature of the alleged infringement, accurately and objectively.

(c) The supervisor shall collect and keep correct records on the case in full.

(d) In terms of its efficacy in rectifying the employee, the suitability of a disciplinary action should be considered.

(e) The defendant's employee should have the opportunity to appeal.

5. Building approach: Disciplinary systems must be preventative rather than punitive to the greatest extent feasible. Instead than imposing sanctions, the focus should be on avoiding breaches.

Discipline should be exercised by the immediate line supervisor. The cause for the action against the employee should be stated as well as how similar sanctions might be avoided.

6. Autonomous discipline: autonomy is the finest kind of discipline and management of employees should promote this feeling of discipline. The supervisor must have a normal attitude towards the worker after taking disciplinary action.

7. Check and Review: The supervisor should perform an unbiased function as a court that enforces the law. He should not be ridiculed, offended and criticised personally.

Industrial fatigue

There is minimal human work capability. Care, focus and concentration are required for any job. For extended durations, a person cannot work constantly. The work performance will decrease more in the morning and over time as a person feels mentally and physically at night. Fatigue is known as a reduction in job efficiency owing to prolonged working durations.

Before industrial engineers, this is one of the most serious difficulties. The definition of fatigue is a negative desire for labour. "Tension, the submission to job specialisation and a rhythm that does not keep a person in check," says vitals, "encourage weariness defined by a drop in working capacity, a reduction in work pressure and increased pleasure from working hours.

Industrial fatigue is the degree of mental and physical exhaustion or depletion of power in an industrial sector caused by bodily or mental effort. Fatigue is not the same as drowsiness, however, fatigue may be related to sleep

Why is this unusual?

1. Today's labour is more educated and conscious of its obligations and rights. Relations with industry – R&I importance.

2. Management must interact with people, as persons with dignity and respect for oneself, not only as components for production. The aim is to transform conventional approaches to management and work, to mutual understanding and cooperation, and to cooperate to accomplish a single

purpose. Good industrial relations have led to industrial peace and productivity growth.

3. Joint staff and management consultations create the path for industrial democracy and help the organisation's progress.

4. Encourage workers to enhance production in conducting industrial interactions. Problems are handled through mutual talks, participation of workers, proposals for proposals, common meetings, etc. Good industrial relations, the efficiency of labour and productivity improve.

5. Management is able to give financial and non-financial incentives to employees with higher productivity

Industrial fatigue importance: Fatigue is a significant phenomenon in industrial psychology, since it generates numerous issues, including stress, fatigue, fatigue, fatigue and of course reduces productivity. Employees identify exhaustion as a sense of discomfort and tiredness; consider it unpleasant and unwanted fundamentally.

Following Tiredness

In both workplaces and out of workplaces, there are several elements that might impact tiredness levels. Lack of restorative sleep is the main cause of tiredness. In conjunction with linked variables, tiredness can also be generated.

The workload is the quantity of work to be done by an employee. It produces occupational tiredness and may be evaluated in 3 categories, including physical load, environmental stress and mental load.

Due to the capacity to take safe judgments, reduced attention spans, poorer memory, lower reactance time and accuracy, fatigue causes employee performance to decline. Fatigue also impacts the attitude and conduct of people. Employees might become impetuous, frequently leading to disputes and misunderstandings. And an overworked workplace has also less empathy, awareness and ethical conduct, which might adversely influence the performance and safety of the company. For instance, if employees don't care about their colleagues, they are less likely to raise safety concerns willingly.

Moreover, tiredness and related physical problems and diseases can lead to short- and long-term job shortages and increased healthcare expenditures. Fatigue causes, last but not least, a considerable productivity loss. A distraction, mistakes and an unable to concentrate may have a bad effect on the basis, which can have an even greater influence on the morale of employees.

Worker Fatigue Reduction Strategy

Resolution of labour weariness is not easy, as every person has distinct repercussions and many people don't even know how extremely tedious they are. Fortunately, companies may apply some fundamental methods to decrease worker tiredness and negative impacts on the workplace.

Sleep and tiredness education: Employers may train employees on excellent sleep practises and beneficial sleep advantages.

Reduce worker tiredness hazards. 1. This requires suitable illumination in the workplaces, adequate noise levels (larger levels of noise cause weariness) and pleasant temperatures (i.e. not too warm).

Provide work spaces to prevent tiredness. Ensuring that employees standing with anti-fatigue slabs and workers sitting have the right ergonomics is two instances for ensuring that a workplace does not create tiredness to the worker.

Pay particular attention to extraordinary or lengthy shifts at work. Since most people struggle to adjust completely to odd shift, make sure that they provide extra breaks and food to give more rest to the workers.

Assist workers in managing their tiredness. Unfortunately tiredness makes its way to the work-place, regardless of the amount you learn of the fatigue or how many anti-fatigue techniques are utilised. Some experts are even recommending nap installations since it is proved to enhance employees morality and productivity during a fast sleep of 10-15 minutes.

Leadership

Leadership is the process where one may encourage and inspire others to follow them.

Leadership features are a key element of the perception and operation of a leader. Since leadership is so essential, it is researched and discussed extensively.

For a company, management is highly essential. Top leaders help an organisation to develop morality. Even in difficult circumstances, the efficient leaders of their subordinates may enable them to remain confident and joyful. Great leaders help keep workers.

What is the conduct of leadership?

The leading conduct is the characteristics and features that make a leader effective. Leaders use their conduct to guide, steer and influence their team's work. There are numerous natural traits that increase leadership behaviour, but leaders may build methods and activities to improve and make them more successful. Organisations flourish on leaders who share a vision, motivate teams and guarantee the efficiency of everyone.

Successful leaders' key attitudes and behaviours:

Being a leader effectively covers several things, from knowledge and experience to planning and strategy.

It's how effectively you communicate with people and what kind of connections you establish if you want to stand out as a leader.

Excellent leaders provide more than corporate expertise and strategy. You may develop confidence and empower people with whom you work. Their abilities are what distinguishes them from an inferior leadership model in a better league

1. Good communication

This mindset must be one of the most important impacts on the job.

As a leader, your impact is important.

You will establish the tone of your leadership when you decide to celebrate, encourage or control and criticise

2. Thank you.

A leader who takes time to recognise their employees' hard work will develop a strong and trust-based team.

On the other side, those leaders who scream instructions with no gratitude will not gain confidence or respect for the contribution that someone else does.

3.Come together with the team

While it is good to be vulnerable and let your team know that you are a person, seeing others' weaknesses and bringing your employees together are equally important.If gossip or disagreement takes place, a strong leader will let others know that gossip or little dispute has no place.Each team member is recognised and respected in a healthy environment

4. Enabling and developing others

Successful leaders quickly communicate and do their utmost to empower others. They want their team members to develop their leadership and professional abilities.

5. Make yourself responsible

One who takes steps forward and assumes responsibility each time is a clear indicator of a successful leader.

Nothing is worse than a leader who steps aside and lets one of her team members be held responsible for a miserable circumstance or result.A good leader takes a bit more than his share of the credit, just little less. - Glasow – Arnold H.

6. Empathy Display

An effective leader is emotionally intelligent. They comprehend, even in disagreement with, where the other person comes from.

Empathy for members of employees is important to the healthy culture and pleasure of the workplace.It is understandable to all of us; a successful leader recognises this and makes sure it occurs.

Moral maintenance

The morale of employees does not only represent the happiness of your workers. It directly reflects the health of your culture, the quality of communications between you and the other management and the effectiveness of your managers.

High moral standards are only applied when employees believe their company is taken care of. And since this year has been packed with unpleasant diversions, it is more vital than ever for your staff to have the assistance they need to make their best job each day.

The fundamental problem is how employee morality is maintained.

1. Foster feedback

Openness and transparency are two important elements that contribute to constructive transformation. You will most certainly provide regular feedback on your employees‘ performance, so why do you not provide them feedback too? Fostering feedback may also lead to possible breakthroughs, since new ideas come continuously.

2. Recognition of employees a habit

It is simple to recognise the hard work and accomplishments of an employee. But the impact on productivity and retention may be substantial. Acknowledged employees inspire them to do their job, and if better recognised 69 percent of employees will work more.

3. Consider flexible timing

The way most employees see the balance between work and life has changed fundamentally. The vast majority of millennia value and many even require a flexible schedules.

With flexible timing choices such as telecommuting, shorter workweeks or reductions in hours, the morals of employees may have a significant effect and make the team considerably happy.

4. Provide opportunities for development

Nobody wants to be locked in a dead-end job with no chance of progress. This is a formula for low moral standards and huge sales. Ideally, internally promote where devoted individuals may work up the ladder.

5. Build a Play Element

To stop work and replenish your batteries, everyone has to have some inactive time. One method to make this easier and retain employee morality is to provide your staff an opportunity to "play" in breaks. Google, for example, offers tables and video games for their employees. This was a great method for staff to relax from intensive development sessions.

6. Use correct instruments

It might seem a little intimidating to make employee morals a priority for your organisation with all the information we have given. Studies, however, show that a good work culture leads to higher productivity than others.

Motivation Systems

the system of motivation is a word describing one of its management tools. It comprises of intentionally selected motivators, all of whom are linked; by encouraging workers to certain behaviour and practises they meet the assumptions and mission of the firm.

Company motivation

Proceeding by encouraging staff at three stages we may differentiate if relationships are built on a rewarding incentive system:

1. Motivation for earning (bonuses, raises in wages, perks)

2. Motivation for non-educated material (health programs, insurances, company gadgets, conferences, special trainings)

3. Motivation for non-learning non-materials:

• Organizational - opportunities for promotion, authority, better access to information

• Psychological and social – praises, self-realization, job security

• Technical – better ware work, help.

In addition to these encouraging devices, one of the motivators of businesses is also the working environment itself. Every employee benefits from favourable working conditions, decent corporate locations, good working equipment and a solid business scenario which means less stressful work.

Payment Of Wages

The major aim of the Payment of Salaries Act of 1936 is to eliminate needless delays in paying wages and prevent unlawful wage deductions.

Payment of salaries applicability law

In accordance with Section 1(6) of the Law, earnings below INR 6 500 per month are covered and protected by the Act. The wages are subject to the Law. Furthermore, as set out in the Payment of Wages Act, the law applies to payment to employees working in factories, on trains or in other establishment.

Wages definition

The word wages is defined as all payable to a person hired for his employment or for labour done in such a job (either in terms of pay, allowances or otherwise). Payment of salaries includes: wages

- Any remuneration payable by way of an award, settlement or an order of the Court of Justice; • Any remuneration to which the employee is entitled, for overtime work or vacation or for any period of time of leave;
- Any additional remuneration payable under the terms and conditions of employment (whether called the bonus or any name);
- Any sum to which the person employed is entitled under any scheme framed under any law for the time being in force, but does not include:
- Any bonus (whether in accordance with profit sharing schemes or otherwise) not payable under the employment terms or payable under any award or settlement between the parties or order of a Court;
- The value of a house or supply of electricity, water, medical care, other amenities or service not included in the calculation;
- Any trip allowance or the value of any travel concession; o Any money which the employee shall pay, by the nature of his job, to offset specific expenditures on him; Any gratuity payable at the time of cessation of work.

Payment and wages due date

Pending the expiry of the seventh day of the last day of the salary period, where there were less than 1000 employed, salaries must, according to the 1936 requirements of the Law on Payment of Labor. In the event of less than 1000 employees, salaries have to be paid prior to the end of the ten days of the final day of the wage period.

In addition, salaries should only be paid on business and not on vacation. If any person's job is terminated, the salaries earned by him or her should be paid by the end of the second day after the end date.

Wages and salaries should only be paid in current currency coins or notes, or both. However, to do so, the employer has to have written permission from the employee by means of a cheque or credit to the bank account.

Salary or wage deductions under the Wage Payment Act

Under the Payment of Earnings Act, the employer is permitted the following deduction from an employee's pay or wages.

• Deduction on absence of duty; deductions on damage or loss to the employed persons' goods;

• deductions on employer's supplies of household lodgings;

• deductions on the supplies and service provided by the employer;

• deductions on recovery of advances or interest and adjustment on overpayment;

• Deducting instructions from the Court or other authorities; • Deducting the deposit of a pre-employed person for a subscription and reimbursement of any advance from any Provide Fund; • Deduction of the co-operative company payment;

In any salary period, the total amount of deductions should not exceed 50% of the employees' salaries. If any deductions for payments to cooperative companies are intended for the full or part of them, the deductions cannot exceed 75%.

Payment or salary delay

In this situation, the authorities may apply if there is delays in paying wages or if any deduction has been made from wages. The list of those who can apply to the authority is as follows:

• A legal practitioner; or

• a registered syndicate officer legally approved in writing;

• an inspector; or

• any other person operating under the power authority authorization.

Personnel Records

Personnel records are records for an organization's employees. The records, factual and complete information relating to records and detention, should be collected. All human resource information in the organisation is systematically kept in order. In numerous decision-making sectors, such records aid a management. For the formulation and examination of staff policies and processes, personnel records should be kept. Every personnel data, such as name, dates of birth, marital status, academic credentials, qualifications of the profession, information of the previous job, etc. are kept for all employee data.

Personnel records types

1. Employment records contain historical records, list sources, progress of employees, medical reports, etc.

2. Logs on wages and salaries comprise information on payroll, pay and wage methods, leave registers, turnover registers and other benefits logs.
3. Training and development includes assessment reports, transfers, training schedules, and techniques of training.
4. Records of health and security contain reports on illness, safety, medical record, insurance, and other information.
5. Service records include the main records of bio-data, residence and family information, academic and matrimonial credentials, prior addresses and records of employment.

Personnel Records purposes

This method is termed a waste of money and effort, according to the opponents of the records of staff. The following are recorded in the personal records: Dale Yoder, an economist at the University of Michigan, USA, has validated the importance of the records of the personnel following a thorough research.

1. It helps to provide managers with critical information on the staff.

2. Keeping a current record of employees' leaves, lockouts, transfers, sales, etc.

3. It allows managers to build different training and development programmes, based on the current circumstances.

4. It assists governments to collect statistics on turnover, absenteeism and other problems relating to staff.

5. It assists managers with modifications of wages, allowances, and other compensation perks.

6. It also supports researchers to carry out a thorough analysis of industrial and market goodwill relations of the company.

CHAPTER VI

Role of Engineer and Technician in the Industry and in Society

Introduction

A person using scientific knowledge for the design, construction and maintenance of engines and machinery or buildings like roads, railroads and bridges is an engineer. An engineer is the person in charge of maintaining a ship's engine while at sea.

An engineer utilises science, technology and mathematics to solve issues. We can observe engineering around us across the world, enhancing our working, moving, communicating, remaining healthy and having fun.

Engineer

Definition:

- *A person whose work is, in accordance with scientific principles, to design or manufacture machinery, engine equipment, or equipment such as streets, roads or bridges:*
- *A civil technician*
- *An engineer for mechanics and structures*
- *Software developer*

The engineering industry now provides more employment opportunities than any other field! Four primary engineering industries have formerly existed: mechanical, chemical, civil and electrical.

The number of engineering degrees available nowadays is enormous. There are six primary engineering industries, and there are hundreds of distinct subcategories in each branch, including mechanical, chemical, civil, electrical, management and geotechnical.

Technician

Definition:

• *A technician is someone whose profession requires expert practical work, for instance in a laboratory, using scientific equipment.*

• *A proficient individual in mechanical, industrial or in a specific technological sector*

• *A worker hired for practical work at a laboratory, technical institution or scientific facility*

• *A person with a particular creative or technical competence, particularly without unique flare or brilliance*

A technician is a technologist with a somewhat practical comprehension of the theoretical concepts and with knowledge of the corresponding skills and procedures. Experienced technicians in a certain field usually have a mid-term grasp of theory and technical expertise. As such, the technical skills of technicians are typically considerably greater than the ordinary layperson and also general experts in this sector of technology. For instance, while audio technicians are not as acoustic as acoustic engineers, they do know more about sound equipment and would probably know more about acoustics than others such as actors. Technicians might be categorised as highly qualified or semi-qualified employees, and they could be included in a broader process. They may be located in a number of sectors and they generally have a job title that follows the category of work with the term 'technician.'

The utilisation of established scientific ideas and rules is initiated by engineering. Joined with several practical efforts. Solving his basic wants by trying to develop practical instruments for improving his earthly life. Early scientists were compelled to plunge into the actual inventions of engineering, which have finally transformed our present world.

Over the years, the engineering community started to evolve that so many modifications in the processes of manufacturing began in the early XIXth century. Then the UK engineers could develop a basic steam-driven machine. i.e. the motor steam. This basic development in British technology has given the government as a whole enormous profit. There have been so many improvements in production. In turn, this strengthened the nation's economic power. All industries grew up soon as their new machines were now allocated to work. The transport, power and other fundamental sectors of the economy of the nation rapidly turned to the steam engine, which enhanced their economy in return. The engine was utilised for energy generation and also for transporting caravans. Over time, this development expanded around the globe and eventually engineering found wider grounds for use.

You will witness instances of engineering which have a beneficial impact on everyday life everywhere you turn. Cars are safer, the acoustics are improved by sound systems, precise medical checks and much more fun for computers and cell phones! You will give your community back.

World Change:

Imagine what life might look like without environmental pollution regulations, life-saving medical equipment or cheap building materials in order to combat global poverty. All of this requires engineering. Engineers save lives, prevent illness, alleviate poverty and safeguard our planet in very real and concrete ways.

Revolution:

The earliest technicians focused on military technology, arms like swords and catapults, and robust medieval fortresses. Subsequent engineers created highways, bridges, dams, power lighting, internal fuel engines, computers - the luxuries of our contemporary existence. In the 21st century, the engineers of today have resolved issues, cleaned up the environment with plants and microorganisms, produced cars and trucks with biofuels, designed the vehicles and trucks we drive to work and school, and improved our world of life.

What is an Industrial Engineering Technician?

The technicians are involved in research, evaluation, design and quality control procedures alongside the engineers. They can be engineered in civil, mechanical, industrial, computer, aeronautical, or environmental technology. Engineering technicians are responsible for any duties the engineer assigns, and can create reports and update records.

Job Description of Engineering Technician

Industrial engineering professionals help the industries and production facilities in their productivity, safety and efficiency with the application of engineering techniques and concepts. Industrial engineering experts assist in implementing ideas to make materials, machinery and employees more efficient and effective. They plan workflow, perform research, develop equipment and layouts and assess the expenses of manufacturing.

Many industrial engineering technicians serve as industrial engineering assistants, conduct equipment inspections and testing according to the orders of their superiors.

Responsibilities of Field Service Technicians include:

- Provide client support and support for field trips or shipments
- Schedule workflow
- Manage all installation, repair, maintenance or test jobs at the site
- Diagnostic mistakes or technical issues and find the appropriate remedies

- Document Processes
- Safe operation of vehicle and use of field automation technologies
- Produce timely and thorough service reports

Follow the processes and guidelines filed by all companies

- Cooperate and share information within the organisation with a technical team
- Understand client requirements and provide suitable recommendations
- Build strong customer connections

Requirements

- Proven expertise in field service
- Function to troubleshooting, testing, repair and maintenance of technical equipment
- Flexible shift skills and adaptation
- Familiarity with mobile tools and software
- Technical degree or certification.

Technician Vs Engineer: Differences

In fact, while technicians and engineers typically work together for effective project completion, equipment maintenance and security measures, the two professions vary. The differences are the most common:

Technicians assist in their tasks engineers, while engineers supervise staff and manage projects.

Project layouts are developed by technologists while project development is carried out by technicians.

Typically, just high school or associate diplomas are necessary for technicians, whereas minimum bachelor's degrees are required for engineers.

Engineers base their work on industrial theories while technicians focus more on the practical implementation by the engineers of the ideas.

- Engineers focus more on issue solving whereas technologists focus more on executing the necessary modifications to resolve the problem.
- Engineers are generally higher than technicians because of their higher education level.
- Team management teams or leaders are engineers and monitor work by technicians and other team members.
- Project plans for commerce and public safety can legally be approved by the engineers. This power or the capability to approve plans is not available to technicians.

Technician's tasks and duties

What are a technician's duties?

Although a technician's tasks vary based on his sector and area of work, many technicians have common responsibilities:

- Use drawing and schematics tools and software to create layouts
- ·Working with engineers to guarantee efficient production
- Using software 3D for the processing of components and equipment together
- Install and test new products
- Check blueprints to verify accurate work or project requirements
- Provide customer assistance and answer goods and equipment inquiries
- Provide issue-solving on products and equipment, and repair when appropriate
- Ensure that goods satisfy the criteria for safety and quality control
- Solutions for the development and testing of technological challenges
- Support in goods, services or equipment research and development

What is a technician's responsibility?

- Together with engineers to develop, construct and test solutions for a range of technological challenges.
- Control and alteration of existing prototypes and designs.
- Research, data collection and daily reporting.
- CAD software is used to produce engineers' designs and feedback.
- Communicate with project managers and customers to discuss the project requirements, to plan and to prepare for the essential project completion procedures.
- Create draughts providing specifics on the layout and the required information for the project to ensure the accuracy of all calculations.
- To calculate precisely material needs to reduce waste, do the necessary calculations on the size and component specifications of each project.
- Tests, diagnoses and calibrations are performed.
- Experiments and research are conducted under Engineers' direction.
- Inventory inspection and rearranging of technical components and materials.
- Analysis of operations and improvement ideas.
- Records maintenance and presentation support.

- Participation in conferences and other opportunities for education and advancement.
- Analyse reports to verify that the projects are on time and within budget, and make necessary changes as needed to reach each benchmark on the project.
- Regular quality control controls are carried out to verify that every project part complies with the company's high requirements.
- Development of new ideas, or revision of established methods, to make the best quality goods more efficient.
- Coordinate with personnel in other departments as needed, so they will continue to be informed of their anticipated tasks and all project components will work well.

Foreman

Foreman's meaning:

The term "supervisor" denotes something like a supervisor who acts as a connection between front-line and top management personnel. From beginning to completion, they supervise production and construction projects. Foremen study designs, monitor the work being carried out and verify that safety rules are complied with.

The boss is the most important and effective position between managers and employees. He is directly responsible for the work and oversees the operations in his area.

It is responsive to the individual and collective efforts of the man group and is also capable of achieving outcomes in terms of both quality and quantity as anticipated. He must guide his soldiers and inspire them and must be acquainted with human psychology and the art of men.

Other tasks and duties centre on project management and do what it takes to achieve a job. They employ, train, oversee and assess employees. Daily attendance and reprimands are checked rigorously to ensure that the whole team remains on a tight schedule when necessary. Ranking employees realise that a contractor is business while placing orders and establishing deadlines.

A position as a master also involves continuous connection with building managers that supervise the broader picture. Progress reports, schedules projected and budgetary updates are provided by forecasts. They may discuss how to deal with personal concerns, like as overtime and leave requests, pursuant to any applicable collective bargaining agreements with project unions.

Foreign Office (Supervisor) duties:

I. towards management :

1. Management policies to be transposed into employees.
2. Inform the management about emplcyees' wishes.
3. Time to obtain the necessary production.
4. To preserve the quality standard.
5. Formulate production efficiency planning and methodologies.
6. Minimization of wastes.
7. Proposals whenever necessary.
8. Act between staff and employers as a middle man.

II.Towards the workers under him:

Monitoring is considered direct and instant supervision and management of subordinates. The supervisor is called a supervisor. The supervisor. The supervisor's obligations to subordinates are:

Provide the appropriate instructions on.

(a) Company policies and procedures.

(b) The correct operational approach.

1. Cleanliness, safety, etc. to maintain good working conditions.
2. Keep discipline.
3. Promoting goodwill and cooperation initiatives.
4. Representing the managerial employees.
5. Encouraging and crediting proposals, when appropriate.
6. Impartially encourage and transfer.
7. Leading his soldiers and inspiring them.
8. Each employee is best matched to the task.
9. He is going to function as a buddy, philosopher, and workers' mentor.

III. **Towards the other foremen:**

1. Keep cordial and helpful relationships.
2. Keep working flows from other departments and to others.
3. Remove and withstand any departmental influence.

IV. towards the work

1. To help pick appropriate materials.
2. Choose the optimum equipment for a particular job.
3. Minimizing material waste.
4. Report on job progress, work spoilage, and machine and operation waste.

5. Management cooperation has been shown to be important for improvements in tactics, ways of compensation, and working conditions.

6. Make suggestions with regard to accident hazard precautions.

7. Aid to the department of training.

8. Keep the records needed.

9. Know procedures of first-aid.

Engineering is finally starting to employ established scientific theories and rules. Joined with several practical efforts. Solving his basic wants by trying to develop practical instruments for improving his earthly life. Early scientists have been compelled to dig into actual breakthroughs from technology, which have finally transformed our world today. Industrial engineering professionals help the industries and production facilities in their productivity, safety, and efficiency with the application of engineering techniques and concepts. Industrial engineering experts assist in implementing ideas to make materials, machinery, and employees more efficient and effective. Depending on the business, and industrial engineering technician may have several distinct tasks. One aspect of the work is typically to contribute to the development, evaluation, and improvement of processes. They may be involved in the establishment and design of procedures and standards, the preparation of equipment and machinery layouts, or the troubleshooting and solutions to quality control issues. You may also check and record time, movement, method, and speed activities for the purpose of determining or improving production rates. Technicians of industrial engineering operate in different industries, while nevertheless performing the same core tasks. Industry engineering technology companies may employ plants, offices, shops, repair shops, health centers, and sites of waste disposal.

CHAPTER VII

Industrial Safety And House Keeping

Magnitude and Cost of Accidents Cause of Accidents

What is it?

The process of uncovering the fundamental causes of accidents, on-the-job injuries, property damage, and near calls in order to prevent them from happening again is known as accident investigation.

Why it is Important?

Accident investigation will bring you to the true cause of what happened, and once you have that information, you may take proactive steps to avoid future accidents.

What is required?

Develop an accident investigation process that focuses on:

- fact-finding, not fault finding
- determining the root causes of why the event occurred
- Make changes so the event does not happen again.
- Set a policy that all accidents and close calls (big and little) will be thoroughly examined.
- Staff conducting accident investigations should be given training and instruments.
- Audit completed investigations to ensure that they are finished on schedule and with sufficient depth.

How do you do it?

Accidents in the workplace should be investigated as quickly as feasible. The goals of a timely and thorough accident investigation should be to:

- determine the accident's cause
- prevent a recurrence of the accident
- improve working conditions in terms of health and safety
- assess whether the accident was caused by a violation of federal or state safety and health regulations.
- decide if a firm or an individual is liable in the event of future legal action
- assess whether damaged objects need to be repaired or replaced

- Identify the need for increased personnel education and training.

A thorough and complete accident investigation involves several steps, specifically:

- background investigation
- site investigation
- interviews
- analysis and reporting.

The following overview goes over each of these processes in greater depth.

Background Investigation

- Examine any injured employees' and/or others' employment and injury records who may have contributed to the accident.
- Examine any injury reports as well as any damage to equipment, machines, buildings, or property.
- Make a list of anyone who witnessed the accident.
- Gather information about the area's regular circumstances and/or operations. Maps, floor layouts, wiring diagrams, and any other pipe or architectural drawings or operational guidelines would be included in the information.
- area to outline the purpose and goals of the investigation. Ensure that there is a basic understanding of the materials, equipment, operation, or process involved.
- Meet with the supervisors and other employees in charge of the impacted area, as well as employees from the affected company.

Site Investigation

- Arrive at the accident location as quickly as possible when the occurrence occurs.
- During the site investigation, restrict access to the accident scene to authorised personnel.
- To prevent tampering or other alterations, make sure any mobile evidence is secured.

- Determine whether any physical changes have occurred as a result of the accident. Clean-up, weather, maintenance, and typical usage could all play a role in the changes.
- Tour the entire area and take notes on your initial impressions of the structure, gardens, equipment, lighting, and ventilation.
- Sketch or draw parts of the accident scene where equipment or machinery involved in the accident is located or where actions that contributed to the accident occurred.
- Parts of the accident scene where equipment or machinery involved in the accident is located, or where acts that contributed to the accident occurred, should be sketched or drawn. When sketching or drawing an accident scene, keep the following criteria in mind:

1. Use graph (squared) paper. Determine the value for each square and record it at the bottom of each sketch if distance or size are essential.
2. Each sketch should be oriented with an arrow pointing north.
3. Label all objects.
4. Individual and/or vehicle travel paths should be indicated with arrows.
5. Indicate the distance between two fixed positions for mobile items.
6. Make a note of where witnesses who were there at the time of the accident were.

- Take pictures of the entire site, any damaged locations, and any relevant apparatus or equipment. Before any changes are made to the accident scene, photographs should be taken.

1. Check to see if the area has been altered before snapping photos. Do not return things that have been relocated or modified for pictures. Photograph the things as they were found, but also capture the change and the person who was responsible for or aware of the change.
2. To identify the size or slope of the items shot in close-ups, utilise reference items such as a ruler or level measurer. To offer a reference, photograph the identical thing from a distance for each close-up. Take pictures of the area where the wounded worker(s) were discovered, using reference markers to show where they were.

Interviews

- Make a list of witnesses and other people who should be interviewed.
- Allow no more than 24 hours between conducting interviews if at all possible.
- To prevent interruptions and distractions, do interviews in a private area.
- To prevent interruptions and distractions, do interviews in a private area.
- Prepare a list of questions for any interview in advance. Use questions that demand you to provide a narrative response. Questions that imply an unexpected response should be avoided. (Example: "Isn't it true that the injured employee was running?") or that can be answered with either "yes" or "no".
- Who questions identify all parties involved.

1. What questions identify pertinent actions, events, and physical objects?
2. Where questions locate participants, witnesses, and key objects involved in the accident.
3. When questions determine the time of the accident and establish relationships between pairs of activities or events.
4. How questions provide information on the interaction and relationships among participants, equipment, and the events leading up to, during, and after the accident.
5. Why questions determine unsafe acts or hazardous conditions.

- Before beginning the interview, inform the person being interviewed that the goal of the session is to figure out what caused the accident and how to avoid it happening again.
- Begin the interview by asking the person to explain what happened. Interrupting with inquiries is not a good idea.
- After the person has provided his or her initial statement, ask the prepared questions as well as any additional questions that the person's statement has generated.
- In the order in which they occur, record the individual's statement, the questions asked, and the responses obtained. Allow the individual to speak, but do not allow him or her to ramble. When necessary, interrupt to bring the conversation back to the topic at hand.
- When all questions have been addressed and the individual has indicated that no additional information can be shared, end the interview.

Encourage the person to contact you if any other details spring to mind. Review the individual's statement and replies right after the interview and write down your impressions and conclusions.

Analysis and reporting

Analyze the data to discover all causes of the accident after all fact-finding efforts have been completed. Then write a detailed report documenting the discovered causes and describing how to avoid similar mishaps in the future. It's critical to recognise that most accidents have multiple causes in order to better understand why they happened and plan for preventive measures. It's crucial to remember that an accident might occur as a result of the collision of seemingly unrelated events.

Causes

Any behaviour, condition, act, or omission that would have prevented the accident or reduced the severity of the injuries would be considered the cause of the accident. Direct, indirect, or contributing causes can all be classified.

Acts or omissions that are directly related to the accident are referred to as direct causes. These could include workers or other individuals who:

- Use machinery in a dangerous manner, or operate machinery that has known safety flaws or deficiencies
- do not adhere to the necessary or mandated safety safeguards or procedures
- Equipment, machinery, and vehicles with known damage or incorrect operations are not repaired.

Indirect causes are conditions that directly contribute to the occurrence of a direct cause. These causes could include:

- defective or unusual conditions of equipment, machinery, vehicles, buildings, or grounds
- defective or unusual conditions of workers or other individuals, such as intoxication, physical defects or limitations, or psychological defects or limitations

hazardous or unusual conditions of weather.

Conditions, programmes, activities, or omissions that are not directly related to the accident but did contribute to the occurrence or existence of a direct or indirect cause are referred to as contributing causes. These causes could include lack of or inadequate:

- safety program
- training programs
- preventive maintenance programs
- corrective maintenance programs
- supervision
- enforcement
- design of equipment, machinery, vehicles, or facilities
- advisory or warning communication, labels, or signs.

Analysis

Collect and correlate data:

The following are some examples of resources that can be used to determine all of the accident's causes. These documents should be gathered and structured so that investigators can look through all of the data at once.

1. summary of employment and injury records of pertinent employees
2. summary of orientation and training records for pertinent employees
3. summary of normal conditions and/or operation of the pertinent area
4. a description of how to use materials, equipment, facilities, operations, or procedures in a normal and safe manner
5. a summary of the goods, equipment, and facilities that were inspected
6. An outline of areas of agreement and disagreement between witness statements is included in the summary of witness statements.
7. a summary of relevant preventative maintenance or repair records
8. Materials, equipment, buildings, operations, or procedures are covered by written business policies or directives.

Review data and pose hypothetical causes. All relevant data should be reviewed by the investigator. The investigator should identify potential direct, indirect, and contributory causes after the initial review. It is critical that all potential causes be documented, and that the investigator not make any assumptions about whether or not a potential cause was relevant to the incident. It may be beneficial to have a second person perform an independent evaluation of the relevant data in order to identify all possible reasons. Test potential causes. Examine the relevant data once more, looking for particular data that supports or refutes each plausible reason. Connect the reasons that are related to each other, whether they are direct, indirect, or contributing.

Reporting

A written report should be generated that contains the following sections:

Statement of the problem. This section should include:

- a review of the incident
- a summary of injuries, lost time, and equipment and/or property damage.

Review of the data. This section should include:

- a summary of witness statements
- a description of key findings relating to the accident, the affected employees' work history, and the functioning of apparatus or equipment
- a storyboard with photographs or sketches
- An overview of existing, written company policies or directives.

Causes This section should include a list of the data-supported direct, indirect, and contributory factors. The data that supports each cause should be mentioned. .

Recommendations. These should be based directly on each of the noted causes. These recommendations could include the following:

- more or improved training for employees
- new company policies or directives, or better clarification or dissemination of existing ones
- improved communication between employees, supervisors, and management
- design or operation changes or improvements to machines, equipment, or processes
- different or improved safety equipment
- different or improved protection from natural phenomena or disasters

- different or improved systems to account for possible physical, physiological, or psychological limitations of employees, customers, or others.

Job Safety Analysis

What is a Job Safety Analysis

Job Safety Analysis (JSA) is a systematic technique that divides each job/task into important training sequences, identifies safety aspects in each job/task step, and instructs the employee on how to avoid potential safety hazards. A Job Hazard Analysis, or JHA, is another frequent term for this technique. Both a JSA and a JHA are used interchangeably. A specific work assignment, such as "running a grinder," "using a pressurised water extinguisher," or "fixing a flat tyre," is frequently referred to as a "job" or "task."

Some people choose to broaden the scope of the investigation to include all areas of the profession, not just safety. Total job analysis is the term for this method. Safety is an intrinsic aspect of every job, not a distinct entity, according to the methodology. Only health and safety issues will be addressed in this booklet.

Benefits of doing a Job Safety Analysis

Observing a worker perform the job is one of the strategies employed in this case. This method has several advantages, including the fact that it does not rely on individual memory and that seeing or executing the procedure encourages the realisation of potential hazards. Observation may not be feasible for jobs that are performed infrequently or are new.

One method is to have a discussion with a group of experienced workers and supervisors to complete the analysis. One advantage of this strategy is that it involves more people, resulting in a broader base of experience and a more readily accepted work practice. This approach must include members of the health and safety committee.

Four basic steps of JAS

Four basic stages in conducting a JSA are:

1. Selecting the job to be analyzed
2. Breaking the job down into a sequence of steps
3. Identifying potential hazards
4. Determining preventive measures to overcome these hazards

Important to know when "selecting the job"

In an ideal world, every employment would be submitted to a JSA. The amount of time and effort required to conduct a JSA might sometimes be a practical restriction. Another factor to consider is that whenever equipment, raw materials, processes, or the environment change, each JSA will need to be revised. As a result, it's normally important to determine which jobs should be examined. This phase ensures that the most vital occupations are reviewed first, even if an examination of all jobs is planned.

How do I break the job into "basic steps"?

After deciding on a job for analysis, the following step is to break it down into steps. A job step is a piece of an operation that is required to progress the work. Please see the samples below. It's important not to make the steps too broad. It won't help if you skip certain processes and the risks that come with them. On the other hand, if they are very detailed, there will be an excessive number of processes. Most jobs, on average, can be defined in less than ten steps. If more stages are needed, consider splitting the project into two halves, each with its own JSA, or combining processes where possible. This document will take the job of changing a flat tyre as an example.

It's critical to remember to follow the procedures in the exact order. Any step that is not completed in the correct order may miss major potential dangers or add hazards that do not exist.

How do I "identify potential hazards"?

Potential dangers must be identified at each step after the basic steps have been recorded. List the things that could go wrong at each phase based on your observations of the job, your understanding of accident and injury causes, and your personal experience.

It's possible that a second look at the job in progress is required. Because the fundamental stages have previously been documented, more attention can now be paid to each potential danger. At this point, there is no attempt to resolve any issues that have been identified.

To help identify potential hazards, the job analyst may use questions such as these:

1. Can any body part get caught in or between objects?
2. Do tools, machines, or equipment present any hazards?
3. Can the worker make harmful contact with moving objects?
4. Can the worker slip, trip, or fall?
5. Can the worker suffer strain from lifting, pushing, or pulling?

6. Is the worker exposed to extreme heat or cold?
7. Is excessive noise or vibration a problem?
8. Is there a danger from falling objects?
9. Is lighting a problem?
10. Can weather conditions affect safety?
11. Is harmful radiation a possibility?
12. Can contact be made with hot, toxic, or caustic products?
13. Potential hazards are listed in the middle column of the worksheet, numbered to match the corresponding job s

Safety Education System And Visual Aids

Safety Education System

Safety education is a type of education that strives to provide individuals with information and comprehension of safety measures and methods. Individuals must be safe in order to promote good bodily and psychological health and well-being. According to the findings of the study projects. Safety education is a type of education that strives to provide individuals with information and comprehension of safety measures and methods. Individuals must be safe in order to develop healthy physical and psychological health and wellbeing.

Safety education is a type of education that strives to provide individuals with information and comprehension of safety measures and methods. Individuals must be safe in order to promote good bodily and psychological health and well-being. According to study studies, when people feel unsafe, it has negative consequences for their physical and mental health. Individuals need to improve their understanding of a variety of elements in order to increase safety. Additionally, individuals must improve their competences and talents in order to stay safe in a particular environment.

Individuals of diverse ages, categories, and backgrounds must improve their knowledge and understanding of safety education measures. Individuals must promote their own safety both inside and outside their houses. Safety education is a type of education that strives to provide individuals with information and comprehension of safety measures and methods. Individuals must be safe in order to promote good bodily and psychological health and well-being. According to study studies, when people feel unsafe, it has negative consequences for their physical and mental health. Individuals need to improve their understanding of a variety of elements in order to increase safety. Additionally, individuals must improve their competences and talents in order to stay safe in a particular environment. Individuals of diverse ages, categories, and backgrounds must improve their knowledge and understanding of safety education measures. Individuals must promote their own safety both inside and outside their houses.

Safety education

Through the formal and informal curriculum, all school staff, including teaching and non-teaching staff, are responsible for safety instruction. If safety education is to be effective, it must be ingrained in the school's culture and ethos.

What can safety education achieve?

Safety education may help children and young people, as well as their parents and caregivers, implement appropriate safety practices. Young cyclists, for example, can be taught how to plan better routes to avoid the most dangerous intersections. In the event of a fire, installing smoke alarms and practicing escape routes can save lives.

What students learn in school about risk assessment may be applied outside of the classroom, and it can boost receptivity to safety information and guidance from other sources. Safety education can help young people make confident and competent judgments about and participate in a variety of activities, including sports, adventurous activities, travel, and job experience.

What is safety education?

- Students should be able to keep themselves safe and contribute to the safety of others through safety education. It enables people to be aware of potential dangers in various aspects of their lives and to make proper judgments and actions.
- Safety education is about equipping young people to manage properly with a wide range of situations, not about shielding them from all hazards — the bumps, cuts, and bruises that are a normal part of growing up.
- Safety education includes:

Hazard awareness and recognition, as well as risk assessment and management skills. Risk assessment will be taught to students in disciplines including design and technology, science, and physical education. Students can apply what they've learned in safety education to other aspects of their lives. The elements that influence safety-related attitudes and behaviour. Safety education should take into account stereotypes and pressures that promote risk-taking, such as media images equating driving with speed or the influence of fashion trends on protective equipment wear.

Assertiveness and other personal and social skills are vital in allowing students to take responsibility for their own and others' safety, such as when asking for help or calling the police, or when requesting an adult to wear a seat belt or drive more carefully.

The importance of emotions in recognizing and dealing with dangerous situations. Controlling anger, as well as dealing with stress and fear, are important safety abilities.

Contributing to the safety of communities. Learning to accept responsibility for social and moral issues is part of safety education. Discussing safety issues at school and in the community can lead to students participating in efforts to improve safety. It should contain a discussion of social and political concerns that have an impact on the improvement of safety.

Effective planning for safety education will help teachers to promote key skills and thinking skills:

Key skills

- Information technology
- Improving pupils' learning and performance
- Information processing
- Enquiry
- Evaluation thinking skills
- Working with others
- Problem solving.
- Reasoning
- Creative thinking

Most people understand the need of a well-designed safety management education programme, but sadly, not everyone follows it. The ability of a firm to keep its people safe is determined by its ability to create, implement, and improve safety management systems and programmes.

The world's finest firms put employee health and safety first, making it a shared responsibility for everyone. These businesses do so in a systematic approach that allows them to effectively practise preventive while also preparing them to deal with any incident that may arise. According to the National Safety Council, an effective safety management program should:

- Reduce the risk of workplace incidents, injuries, and fatalities through data-driven measurements and improvements
- Involve people from different parts of the organization to make safety a shared responsibility
- Be well organized and structured to ensure consistent growth and performance
- Be proactive, preventive and integrated into the culture of the entire organization

Given those requirements, we assembled a collection of "must haves" from industry leaders to provide you with a guide for creating a top-notch safety management program.

Here are the 8 key components of a successful safety management education program:

1.Formulized safety policies

The first step to achieving safety success is to lay out your company's safety rules, which should include your company's viewpoint on the necessity of safety management as well as the general expectations of each employee for how to act in certain situations.

Employees should embrace and follow important operating knowledge in their day-to-day work lives, according to safety standards. These rules should cover anything from fundamental operating procedures like what to do in the event of a fire to comprehensive instructions for dealing with injuries if someone is injured on the job or while in the building.

2. Effective and regular communication about safety and health

It is critical to have safety policies that are often stated and accessible to everyone. Organizations must discuss safety rules with employees and managers to ensure that they are understood and implemented.

3. Utilization of both leading and lagging indicators

Every safety leader's checklist for safety performance should include the capacity to swiftly and precisely identify high-risk scenarios. Leading indicators can provide insight into what might happen in the future, allowing the company to plan ahead and prevent accidents. Leading indicators include things like the frequency of safety training, the number of and results of safety audits and inspections, and operational behaviours like mean time to corrective action completion, staff involvement in proactive actions, and even leadership involvement.

4. Support for behavior-based safety

The world's safest companies understand the necessity of developing safety practices. That's why many of them focus on behavior-based safety – a safety methodology that focuses on improving safety through habit creation.

5. Frequent safety training and discussion

The world's safest firms understand the importance of continuing education for their staff and make it a priority.

- Knowledge of proper practices to do their job safely
- Awareness of how to eliminate hazards to reduce risk
- Specialization when their specific roles require unique preparation.

These three elements are essential for minimising the number of incidents while also improving overall safety. When it comes to implementing frequent training, one challenge that companies confront is that training sessions can be long and dull.

6. Empowered and motivated employees

Empowering people through your approach to safety management can have a huge impact on the bottom line of your company. Many firms, on the other hand, struggle to attain the appropriate degree of employee engagement.

7. Cutting edge tools and systems

Companies with low injury rates provide their employees with more than simply systems and safety management programmes to help them succeed. They use cutting-edge technologies and processes to ensure that their personnel are prepared for whatever comes their way.

8. Comfort with reporting issues related to safety

It's natural to want to get the job finished on schedule — or even ahead of time — but with a "get it done quick" attitude, accidents happen. Top tier organizations emphasize the importance of reporting potential problems before they occur, or reporting safety incidents the moment they happen.

Keep in mind that the commitment to safety and establishing a safe and healthy culture is never-ending. You will always find areas of opportunity for improvement, new employees to train, new hazards to address and more. These challenges keep the job interesting and rewarding! Through a top-notch safety management program, you'll gain a systematic approach to evaluating, improving, and reviewing your safety activities to increase organizational success.

Visual-aid

Keeping employees' attention while providing the facts they need to remember is a difficulty while giving safety presentations. Employees are frequently drowsy, distracted by coworkers, checking email on their smartphones, texting, or believing they already know everything there is to know about the presentation. Because safety isn't exactly a glamorous subject, visual aids can serve to pique the learner's interest.

The Advantages of Visual Aids for Safety Training

You can use visual aids to help keep your audience's attention by using them. According to studies, up to 65 percent of the population learns best visually and visual function occupies a large section of the brain.

1 The addition of a relevant visual to an oral presentation can greatly help to keep the audiences' eyes focused forward and increase the retention of the material they are being taught.

2 visual-retention

Visual aids can:

- Add clarity to the presenter's message
- Increase the interest of the presenter's information
- Increase the retention level of the presenter's message
- Stimulate the audience's vision
- Enhance the presenter's credibility
- Improve the presenter's persuasion

Types of Visual Aids:

Visual aids come in many forms. All of the following types of visual aids work towards reinforcing the presenter's message as well as keeping the audience engaged.

- Props
- Models of all sizes
- Enlarged photographs
- Illustrations
- Maps
- Diagrams

- Charts and graphs
- Presentation software: PowerPoint, Slide Rocket Pro, Apple Keynote, etc.
- Slides and video footage
- Physical demonstrations by the presenter
- Visual Aids Shouldn't be a Distraction
- Training images

Visual aids that reinforce what the presenter is saying at the time and help keep the audience's train of thought on track are the best. Your audience will be confused and distracted by visuals that are unrelated to the topic at hand. Your viewers will lose focus and begin to worry about the significance of the visual in question, as well as whether they have missed something.

Your visual aids should not be the center of attention. They should not be so distracting that the audience loses focus on what is being stated. They must be balanced with the content, support the material, and keep the audience engaged at the same time.

Safety Training Visual Aid Resources

We've included a link to a library of images to help you add visual aspects to your next safety training presentation. This will help you keep your audience's attention and enhance retention.

1. Introduction:

Education and training have long been recognised as critical components of well-organized workplace health and safety programmes. They are more crucial than ever in today's quickly changing workplace.

Consciousness and attentiveness to safety are developed through safety training and instruction. Safety education cultivates a safety mindset, whereas training aids in the application of gained safety information to a specific job, operation, or procedure. It is a strategy of assisting employees in developing a critical and conscious mind in order to analyse safe work methods or procedures and develop abilities in applying safe methods and practises to their jobs and activities.

The man in the shop is enforcing safety, and his intentional efforts to be safe in all situations and at all times are critical. It's important to remember that people who haven't been taught how to do their tasks properly are more likely to be involved in an accident. It's also true that a well-trained worker is more likely to be a safe worker. As a result, safety awareness must be instilled such that employees' activities and behaviour are regulated by such safety considerations at all times.

This article will go through several aspects of safety training as well as various national and international legislation that apply to safety training, with a focus on the Indian competition.

Many publications, such as books, articles, acts, laws, codes, and standards, were used in the development of this article; but, due to space constraints, the list of these references is not included in this page.

2. Sources of Information:

To give readers a thorough understanding of safety training, it would be beneficial to go through several areas of training, such as sources of safety information, developing training needs, training techniques, and training plans.

The goals of safety information sources relate to four different stages of the accident process.

In the first stage, workers are educated about dangers and persuaded to behave safely using information provided before to the task. Safety training resources, hazard communication programmes, and various types of safety programme materials were used for this purpose.

Education and persuasion methods aim to eliminate not only errors by enhancing worker knowledge and abilities, but also deliberate violations of safety laws by changing unsafe attitudes. Because novice workers are frequently the target audience at this stage, the safety information offered must be more comprehensive than at other phases.

Written procedures, checklists, instructions, warning signs, and product labels can give crucial safety information during routine task execution in the second stage. This information is frequently in the form of concise comments that either advise or remind less trained workers to take the appropriate safeguards. Such statements are frequently included at the proper point within step-by-step instructions outlining how to complete a task. A similar role can be played by placing warning signs in strategic locations. It must be noted that for successful safety communication at this point, a well-trained and motivated workforce is required.

Workers are alerted to aberrant or exceptionally hazardous conditions via highly visible and easily perceived sources of safety information in the third stage. Warning signals, safety markings, tags, signs, lockouts, and other sources of information are among the sources of data. A well-trained and motivated workforce, like in stage two, is required for effective safety communication at this stage as well.

At the fourth stage, workers are focused on completing emergency procedures as quickly as possible during an accident, as well as completing corrective actions as soon as possible after an accident. The locations of exists, fire extinguishers, first aid station, emergency showers, eyewash fountains, and other safety information signs and markings are prominently displayed to communicate facts vital to the proper execution of emergency procedures. Remedial and emergency actions may be specified on product safety labels and MSDSs. A properly trained and motivated workforce, as in stages two and three, is required for effective safety communication at this stage as well.

3. Designing training need:

The employee's position and the sort of job he does in the organisation must be considered while developing training content. The contents should be relevant to the trainee's current work interests and assist him in improving his job performance. It is beneficial to confer with plant or department heads, as well as personnel who will be trained, in order to analyse the job interest and areas of application. This will aid in the restoration of their ecosystem.

It is also critical to ensure that key personnel with special safety and health responsibilities are adequately taught inside the organisation.

Supervisors play a critical role in assuring worker safety and wellness. However, they frequently receive insufficient or no training. As a result, supervisors must be trained in hazard identification and control so that they can take action to remove dangers from their control area. It's important to remember that safety training should be a part of every job's training and specification.

All new starters must be trained in safety and health-relevant to their employment before being assigned in a position where they are at risk or can become a hazard to others, as they are susceptible and more likely to create/meet accidents.

Only by periodically checking if his employees know, understand, and gladly implement safety laws and regulations can a supervisor ensure that they are working conscientiously with safe habits. From induction training through on-the-job training, supervisors must instil a good attitude toward safety. The usage of working space, the position of first aid, housekeeping, and the disposal system, among other things, could be emphasised during the initial training. Safety concerns such as the use of protective equipment and guards, the handling and care of tools, machines, and materials, and safe working procedures should be stressed while presenting details of job instructions.

In order to select the content, it is vital to have a thorough grasp of the learning process, taking into account the trainers' expertise and the trainees' learning capacity.

Comprehensive information on the company's safety policy, activities, and a review of the company's safety performance in terms of year-over-year trends lost man-hours, and damage to goods and equipment, among other things, can assist in emphasizing the importance of supervisors and managers in the implementation and enforcement of safety on the shop floor.

4. Training Methods

Training specialists are frequently confronted with a bewildering array of training approaches to fulfil a specific training goal. It's worth noting that what learners remember from instruction varies from person to person. Many educators believe that the following percentages correspond to what students remember after receiving education.

- 10 % of what is read
- 20 % of what is heard
- 30 % of what is seen
- 50 % of what is seen and heard
- 70 % of what is seen and spoken
- 90 % of what is said while doing what is talked about

Various training methods and approaches are popular. Lecture, discussion, and role-playing techniques are effective in a formal classroom setting for a supervisory or management group. Techniques such as on-the-job instructions and fault analysis are useful for training a small group of shop floor technicians or operatives. At every level, project work and simulation workshops aid learning through application and practice.

The chosen training approach must also keep the pupils' interest. Even if the afternoon courses are at unusual hours, they must be conducted in a group context to maintain their interest.

In general, the approaches employed should assist learners in actively learning the topics. Depending on the type of training, the type of trainees, the availability of time, and the facility provided for training, all of the methods and aids must be employed separately or in combination. The best method (or mix of methods) to use relies on the training goal, learning quality, and desired speed.

5. Training Plans:

Before creating a training plan, it's important to define some general features of training, such as whether the programme is designed to fulfil short-term or present demands or is designed to meet long-term or future needs. It could either be a general education programme or a programme for developing specialised skills. Induction, orientation for new entrants or refreshers, an appreciation event for senior employees, and other types of programmes are possible.

At this point, it's important to determine if the training content chosen can be taught in a structured training programme or conveyed informally through daily interactions.

Informal advice and coaching can be done on an individual basis over time, but formal contributions may be required if the group size grows too large. Induction, orientation, and on-the-job training must all be organised within the organisation and can only be conducted by company employees.

However, the duration of the training should be determined in light of expected outcomes in terms of changes in performance and behaviour, with the goal of providing appropriate coverage to meet the required standard. A part-time programme of no more than 2 hours at a time, on the other hand, might help maintain maintained enthusiasm. For administrative reasons, programmes held outside of or within institutes must be full-time.

A factory-based programme provides the ease of being able to attend to work and be ready when needed. It does, however, suffer from the distraction of being summoned to work. The advantages of a programme away from the workplace include learning continuity, little interruption, trainee motivation, and adequacy of learning through unrestricted exchange of ideas, among others.

Trainers recruited from within the organisation should be knowledgeable in their fields and have a passion for and skill in teaching.

They must be well respected for their position in the organisation and for their authority in the subject, as well as for their demonstrated ability to guide and coach others on safety.

The distinction between training that should be offered by supervisors and training that should be delivered by health and safety specialists is not always clear. Supervisors are more likely to provide job-specific and task-specific training, whereas safety and health specialists are more likely to provide generic training. Regardless matter where this boundary is drawn, today's safety and health professionals must be capable of designing, coordinating, and delivering training.

Persons delivering training should have a full understanding of the topics to be covered, as well as a passion to teach, a professional demeanor and approach, and exemplary behavior that sets a good example. In addition to these qualities, the modem trainer should be familiar with the fundamental concepts of learning.

6. International Scenario

Government regulations in most developed countries mandate that workers receive specific types of safety information. Consider the following scenario:

The Occupational Safety and Health Administration (OSHA) in the United States has issued a Hazard Communication Standard that applies to workplaces that utilise poisonous or hazardous materials and mandates training, container labelling, the distribution of MSDSs, and other forms of warnings. For dangerous compounds, the Environmental Protection Agency (EPA) has devised many labelling standards. The Department of Transportation (DOT) has specific rules for labelling hazardous materials in transportation.

It's worth noting that in the United States, failure to warn can lead to lawsuits holding manufacturers, employers, and others accountable for worker injuries.

The Canadian Centre for Occupational Health and Safety (CCOHS) supports working Canadians' entire well-being, including their physical, psychological, and mental health, by offering information, training, education, management systems, and solutions that support health, safety, and wellness initiatives.

The Health and Safety Executive (HSE) is the national regulator for occupational health and safety in the United Kingdom. It reduces the risk of mortality, injury, and illness at work.

In line with its work, it makes arrangements for and encourages research, publication, training, and information.

Workplace Health and Safety (WHS) rules, formerly known as Occupational Health and Safety (OH&S) laws, govern safety in Australia. Safe Work Australia, on the other hand, is in charge of developing national policies to improve workplace health and safety and workers' compensation in Australia. While it cannot regulate or enforce WHS regulations, it may give education, training, and advice on workplace health and safety, as well as how to integrate safety management into business operations.

A significant number of existing standards offer voluntary suggestions for the use and design of safety data. Multilateral organisations and agencies, such as the United Nations (UN), the European Economic Community (EEC), the International Labour Office (ILO), the International Organization for Standardization (ISO), and the International Electrotechnical Commission (IEC), as well as national organisations, such as the American National Standards Institute (ANSI), the British Standard Institute (BSI), and the International Electrotechnical Commission (IEC), have developed these standards (JISC).

It may be remembered here that Occupational Health and Safety (OHS) training is a pre-requisite for obtaining ISO certifications, such as ISO 9001, ISO 14001, and ISO 45001.

Conclusion:

Workers' understanding of potential dangers and how to avoid them must be raised in order for management to successfully implement an effective accident prevention programme.

For any overall accident prevention programme, safety training and education is a crucial organisational strategy. Employee safety training at all levels is an important company strategy for improving working conditions and the environment via informed cooperation and teamwork. However, in order to identify, organise, and deliver training, such a programme requires the collaboration and commitment of all levels of the organisation.

Employers all across the world provided workers with a wealth of safety information, both to encourage safe behaviours and to discourage risky ones. Modern safety and health experts play an important role in ensuring that all employees, at all levels, receive the proper types and amounts of training. The Safety Officer or Training Officer coordinates this activity and takes the lead in assessing its impact on the overall safety performance of the organisation. The success of these training programmes necessitates senior management's cooperation, support, and active encouragement, as well as departmental heads' appreciation and assistance. It is important to remember that training is an integral part of any organization's efforts to promote a safe, healthy, and productive work environment.

Obligatory Provisions And First Aid

What is first aid?

The provision of rapid medical assistance to someone who has been injured or is ill is known as first aid. Before expert medical help arrives, regular trained people provide first aid.

Workers may require first aid over the course of their workday, thus it is critical that they are trained and equipped to assist their co-workers.

Employers' legal obligations

The minimum first aid requirement in every workplace is:

- a first aid box (including the appropriate equipment);
- a person trained to administer first aid;
- first aid information for all employees.

Every employer in the United Kingdom, regardless of size, is required by law to plan for the provision of first aid at work.

Employers must ensure that someone is ready to provide or organise first aid at all times. If the designated first aider is unavailable for any reason, this applies. A proper first-aid certificate is required of all first responders.

Although it is not required by law that all employers have a fully qualified first aider on staff, someone must be assigned to oversee first aid in the workplace.

First aid assessment

All employers in the UK are required to carry out an assessment of first aid requirements. This assessment should consider:

- whether a designated first aider is required;
- potential hazards in the workplace;
- the size of the company in terms of people and area;
- previous accidents and illnesses;
- hours of working and shift patterns;
- the location of employees during working hours (on or off-site);
- the distance to emergency services;
- potential visitors to the workplace.

First aid box

There is no set requirement for the contents of a first aid box, but as a minimum it should have:

- a leaflet giving general first aid guidance;
- plasters of assorted sizes (20);
- sterile triangular bandages (4);
- disposable gloves (1 pair);
- safety pins (6);
- medium size sterile wound dressings (6);
- large-size sterile dressings (2);
- sterile eye pads (2).

This first aid box is sufficient for most low-hazard workplaces, such as offices. Make sure that all first aid equipment is on date. Tablets and medicines should not be kept in the first aid box.

Special requirements

For several industries, there is particular regulation governing the first-aid requirements. Diving and offshore jobs, for example, both have additional first-aid requirements.

If you're self-employed, you'll need to make sure you have enough first-aid supplies.

If you work from home and undertake low-risk employment, you do not need to provide any first aid equipment beyond what is required for domestic purposes, but you should still examine your first aid needs.

Check to see if your employer has provided adequate and sensible first-aid provisions in the workplace.

Encourage other members to pursue certification as first responders.

Firefighting

The act of attempting to prevent the spread of and extinguish significant undesired fires in houses, vehicles, woodlands, and other structures is known as firefighting. Firefighters put out flames in order to protect people, property, and the environment. Firefighters usually receive extensive technical training. This includes both structural and wildland firefighting. Aircraft firefighting, shipboard firefighting, aerial firefighting, maritime firefighting, and proximity firefighting all require specialised training. The poisonous atmosphere caused by flammable materials is one of the most serious risks involved with firefighting operations. Smoke, oxygen scarcity, high temperatures, and hazardous atmospheres are the four principal threats. Falls and structural collapse are further dangers that can compound the problems that come with working in a toxic workplace. Firefighters wear self-contained breathing apparatus to address some of these dangers.

Reconnaissance is the initial step in a firefighting effort, and it is used to find the source of the fire and identify the specific threats.

Water, fuel or oxidant removal, or chemical flame inhibition can all put out a fire; however, because fires are classed by the materials involved, such as grease, paper, electricity, and so on, a specialised type of fire extinguisher may be required. The classification is determined by the types of fires for which the extinguisher is most suited.

Firefighter duties

The objectives of a fireman are to save lives, defend property, and preserve the environment. A fire can quickly spread and put many lives in peril, but modern firefighting techniques can often prevent disaster. A firefighter's responsibilities may include public education on fire safety and conducting fire inspections of locations to ensure compliance with local fire codes.

Firefighter skills

Firefighting necessitates knowledge of firefighting, rescue, and hazardous materials mitigation. Firefighters must also have or be able to gain knowledge about department organisations, operations, and procedures, as well as the district or city roadway system, in order to do their jobs. They must maintain a minimal level of physical fitness and learn various firefighting jobs in a suitable amount of time.

Fire wardens

There is also personnel appointed as fire wardens, also known as the chief officer, in firefighting. Some may be responsible for fire control in a specific area, direct a crew in the suppression of forest fires, or act as fire patrolmen in a logging area, while others may be responsible for fire control in a specific area, direct a crew in the suppression of forest fires, or act as fire patrolmen in a logging area. During fires or other emergencies, the chief officer is in charge of his firefighters and is supposed to command and control the whole situation while effectively combatting the fire or other disaster.

Chief officers must be able to assess their firefighters, make solid decisions on whether to pull firemen from a fire, and react calmly in emergency situations. A fire department's activities must be directed and all firefighting efforts must be supervised by the chief officer. He must also have a thorough understanding of the city, including the locations of streets, fire hydrants, and fire alarm boxes, as well as the major structures. He must also be familiar with explosives, dangerous chemicals, and the characteristics of materials that burn in buildings, residences, and industrial plants.

Civilians can become licenced as Fire Wardens in some jurisdictions, and some cities mandate specific types of structures, such as high rises, to have a certain number of Fire Wardens. For instance, the city of Houston, Texas, mandates that every high-rise tenant have at least one Fire Warden for 7500 square feet occupied, with a minimum of two Fire Wardens each level. In this case, their responsibilities include investigating any fire alarms (to determine if there is a fire and, if so, the nature of the fire), contacting the fire department, directing the evacuation of the facility, activating or delaying the activation of fire suppression equipment such as halon and sprinklers (delayed in the case of a false alarm), meeting the fire department and transporting them to the location of the fire, and meeting and transporting the fire department to the location of the fire.

Hazards caused by fire

The hazardous atmosphere created by combusting materials is one of the most serious risks involved with firefighting operations. Smoke, which is growing more dangerous due to the increased variety and number of synthetic home products, an oxygen-deficient environment (21 percent O2 is typical, and 19.5 percent O2 is considered oxygen insufficient), elevated temperatures, and poisonous atmospheres are the four major risks. To avoid smoke inhalation in such situations, firefighters wear a self-contained breathing apparatus (SCBA; an open-circuit positive pressure device). These aren't oxygen tanks (oxygen, as a powerful fire accelerant, poses a serious risk when mixed with nearly anything combustible in the presence of fire), but they do use compressed air in the same way that SCUBA diving gear does. Depending on the size of the tank and the rate of consumption during intensive activity, a firefighter's SCBA can contain 30 to 45 minutes of air. While this equipment helps to reduce the hazards, firefighters are nevertheless exposed to smoke, poisonous dust, gases, and radiation, which have been linked to a 14 percent increased risk of cancer among firefighters. Even without direct contact with the flames (direct flame impingement), obvious concerns connected with the vast heat created by a fire, such as conduction heat and radiant heat, can inflict significant burns even from great distances. Burns from hot gases (e.g., air), steam, and hot and/or poisonous smoke are among the comparable serious heat-related dangers. Long periods of intensive exercise in hot areas put firemen at risk for health problems including rhabdomyolysis. As a result, firefighters are outfitted with personal protection equipment (PPE) such as Nomex or polybenzimidazole fibre (PBI) fire-resistant clothes and helmets that prevent heat transmission to the body. No piece of personal protective equipment, on the other hand, can totally shield the user from the consequences of all probable fire scenarios. Heat can cause flammable liquids in tanks to burst violently, resulting in what is known as a BLEVE (boiling liquid expanding vapour explosion). Some chemical compounds, such as ammonium nitrate fertilisers, have the potential to explode, resulting in explosion or shrapnel damage. Enough heat causes human flesh to burn as fuel or the water within to boil, posing a risk of serious medical complications. Backdrafts are another potential danger. When a considerable amount of oxygen is added to an oxygen-depleted fire, backdrafts occur. If a fire has been compartmentalised and most or all of the oxygen has been burnt away, opening a window or door poses a significant risk of backdraft. When you add oxygen to a low-burning fire, it will ignite all of the oxygen along the way, which can be disastrous. It has a concussive blast that adds to the effect and can be heard from kilometres away. On the fireground, firefighters must maintain constant communication since one damaged window at the wrong time might cause significant injury to everyone working on the structure. Burns can happen in a fraction of a second, depending on the heat of the fire. Additional fire concerns include smoke obstructing vision, which could lead to a fall or confusion; becoming trapped in a fire; and building collapse.

Reconnaissance and "reading" the fire

The first step in a firefighting effort is reconnaissance, which involves looking for the source of the fire (which may not be clear in the case of an inside fire, especially if there are no witnesses), identifying any unique threats, and detecting potential casualties. A fire in an open area may not necessitate reconnaissance, but a fire in a cellar or underground parking garage with only a few millimetres of visibility may necessitate extensive reconnaissance to locate the source of the fire. The examination of signals of thermal phenomena such as flashover, backdraft, or smoke explosion by firefighters is known as "reading" a fire. It is used during scouting and firefighting operations. The major indicators are: hot zones, which can be identified with a gloved hand by feeling a door before opening it, for example; Soot on windows indicates incomplete combustion and, as a result, a lack of air in the room; Smoke flowing in and out around a door frame, as if the fire were breathing, usually indicates that there isn't enough oxygen to maintain combustion. To evaluate the heat of the smoke, spray water on the ceiling in short pulses of a diffused spray (e.g., a cone with an opening angle of 60°): If the temperature is moderate, the water drips down in drops with a rain-like sound; if the temperature is high, the water vaporises with a hiss—a harbinger of an oncoming potentially deadly flashover. Reconnaissance should ideally include examining a building plan that includes information on structures, firefighter hazards, and, in some cases, the best methods and tactics for fighting a fire in that environment.

Use of water

Spraying a fire with water is a frequent method of putting out a fire. Water serves two purposes: When it comes into contact with fire, it vaporises, displacing oxygen (the amount of water vapour is 1,700 times more than liquid water, and it expands over 4,000 times at 1,000 °F (538 °C). As a result, there isn't enough combustible agent in the fire, and it goes out. Water vaporisation absorbs heat and cools smoke, air, walls, and items that could act as additional fuel, preventing one of the ways fires spread, which is by "jumping" to surrounding heat/fuel sources to start new fires, which then join. Water extinguishment is thus a combination of "asphyxia" (oxygen deprivation) and cooling. Asphyxia suppresses the flame, but cooling is the most critical aspect of controlling a fire in a confined space. Water can be obtained via a pressurised fire hydrant, pumped from water sources such as lakes or rivers, transported by tanker truck, or dropped from water bombers, which are aircraft that have been converted to tankers for combating forest fires. Where access to the region is difficult, an armoured vehicle (firefighting tank) may be deployed.

Asphyxiating a fire

The use of water is not always ideal. This is because some chemical compounds react with water to produce harmful fumes or even burn (e.g., sodium); see water-reactive chemicals for more information. Another issue is that some items, such as hydrocarbons (gasoline, oil, and alcohol), float on water, allowing the fire to spread a burning layer. When a pressurized gasoline tank is threatened by fire, it's critical to avoid heat shocks that could damage the tank if it's sprayed with cooling water; the following decompression could result in a BLEVE (boiling liquid expanding vapour explosion). Water cannot be used to put out electrical fires because water can function as a conductor. In such circumstances, the fire must be put out via asphyxiation. This can be accomplished in a number of ways. To put an end to the combustion, chemical products that react with the fuel can be used. The fire hose can apply a coating of water-based fire-retardant foam to separate the oxygen in the air from the fuel. It's possible to employ carbon dioxide, halon, or sodium bicarbonate. Covering the flame with a fire blanket can cut off oxygen passage to the fire in the case of very tiny fires and in the absence of additional extinguishing agents. Putting a lid on a stove-top pan and leaving it there is a simple and usually efficient approach to put out a fire.

Tactical ventilation or isolation of the fire

Smoke is one of the most dangerous aspects of a fire because it carries heat and hazardous substances while also obscuring visibility. Two distinct tactics may be implemented in the event of a fire in a closed place (building): The fire must be isolated or ventilated. "By 'pulling' fire away from imprisoned humans and things, ventilation promotes life safety, fire extinguishment, and property conservation when employed appropriately. A 4x4 foot aperture is cut into the roof right over the fire room in most structural firefighting situations. This permits heated smoke and gases to escape the area through the aperture, restoring normal conditions within. Because the opening of a ventilation hole gives extra air, and hence oxygen, to the fire, it is critical to coordinate ventilation with an interior fire assault. Ventilation can also help to "limit fire spread by diverting fire toward neighbouring openings, allowing firefighters to safely tackle the fire," as well as reduce smoke, heat, and water damage. The use of a fan to create excess pressure in a portion of the building is known as positive pressure ventilation (PPV). This pressure drives smoke and heat out of the structure, making rescue and firefighting efforts easier. It is vital to have a smoke exit, to be familiar with the building plan so that you can predict where the smoke will flow, and to wedge or prop open the doors that allow for air. The biggest danger of this strategy is that it may hasten the fire or perhaps cause a flash-over, such as if smoke and heat build-up in a dead-end. Hydraulic ventilation is the process of using a fog pattern to guide a stream of water from the inside of a structure out the window. This will effectively remove the smoke from the room. Smoke ejectors could potentially be employed in this situation.

BIS

Bureau of Indian Standards

India's National Standard Body is the Bureau of Indian Standards (BIS). BIS is in charge of ensuring the smooth operation of standardisation, marking, and quality certification activities, as well as matters related to or incidental to these activities.

BIS has benefited the national economy through its core activities of standardisation and conformity assessment by providing safe, reliable, and quality goods; minimizing health hazards to consumers; protecting the environment, promoting exports and imports as substitutes; and controlling the proliferation of varieties, among other things. Apart from benefiting consumers and industry, the BIS standards and certification scheme also supports numerous public policies, particularly in the areas of product safety, consumer protection, food safety, environmental protection, building and construction, and so on.

Through its standards and certification efforts, BIS has worked to address many national goals and other government initiatives such as Swacch Bharat Abhiyan, Digital India, Make in India, and ease of doing business in recent years. BIS continues to address challenges such as technological improvements, climate change, environmental and energy conservation, health and safety, and trade facilitation in the formulation of standards. In the domain of conformity assessment, BIS is aiming to simplify and speed up the processes.

Statutory Framework

The Bureau of Indian Standards Act, 2016, has been implemented since 12 October 2017. The highlights of the new BIS Act are:

Positions BIS as the National Standards Body.

Allows multiple conformity assessment schemes in line with global practices.

Allows the government to appoint any agency other than BIS to certify and enforce standard compliance.

Allows the government to certify items on the basis of health, safety, the environment, national security, and the avoidance of deceptive tactics.

Allows the government to make hallmarking of precious metal items a legal requirement.

Provides consumer protection measures such as product recalls for non-conforming standard labelled products, consumer compensation, and more rigorous penalties.

Objectives Of Bis

Harmonious development of the activities of standardization, marking and quality certification of goods

To give a boost to standards and quality control in order to help the sector expand and flourish while also meeting the expectations of consumers.

Organizational Network

BIS has its Headquarters at New Delhi. It has 5 Regional Offices (ROs) located at Kolkata (Eastern), Chennai (Southern), Mumbai (Western), Chandigarh (Northern) and Delhi (Central). Under the Regional Offices are the Branch Offices (BOs). Ahmedabad, Bengaluru, Bhubaneswar, Bhopal, Chandigarh, Chennai, Coimbatore, Dehradun, Delhi, Durgapur, Faridabad, Ghaziabad, Guwahati, Hyderabad, Jaipur, Jammu, Jamshedpur, Kochi, Kolkata, Lucknow, Mumbai, Nagpur, Parwanoo, Patna, Pune, Raipur, Rajkot, and Vishakhapatnam are among the 33 BO The BOs act as a vital link between the region's state governments, companies, technical institutes, consumer groups, and so on.

Activities

The activities of BIS can be broadly grouped under the following heads:

1. Standards formulation
2. International activities
3. Product Certification
4. Hallmarking
5. Laboratory services
6. Training services - National Institute of Training for Standardisation
7. Consumer Affairs and Publicity

Standards Formulation

Chemicals, Food and Agriculture, Civil, Electro-technical, Electronics & Information Technology, Mechanical Engineering, Management & Systems, Metallurgical Engineering, Petroleum Coal & Related Products, Medical Equipment and Hospital Planning, Textile, and Transportation are among the 14 departments that make up the Bureau of Indian Standards. There are fourteen Division Councils that correspond to these Departments. A number of Sectional committees work under each Division Council. The standards encompass a wide range of industries and assist businesses in improving the quality of their goods and services.

International Activities

International Organization for Standardization (ISO)- ISO is the world's leading developer of voluntary International Standards and is an independent, non-governmental membership organisation. BIS is a founding member of ISO and is actively involved in the creation of International Standards by serving on numerous Technical Committees, Sub-Committees, Working Groups, and other bodies as a Participating (P) or Observer (O) member.

International Electro-technical Commission (IEC)- The International Electrotechnical Commission (IEC) was established in 1906 and is the world's premier body for the development and publication of international standards in all electrical, electronic, and related technologies. BIS is India's representative in the IEC.

Consumer Affairs And Publicity

Through numerous awareness programmes, BIS aims to raise awareness and promote quality among all of its customers:

Consumer Awareness Programmes: Consumer awareness programmes are held on a regular basis by various BIS Regional and Branch offices, sometimes in collaboration with Consumer Organizations, to promote the concept of standards, certification, and quality consciousness among consumers.

Industry Awareness Programmes: Industry Awareness Programmes are held by BIS to spread the notion of standardisation, product certification, management system certification, and other BIS initiatives among industries.

Educational Utilization of Standards Programmes: BIS organises Educational Utilization of Standards Programs (EUS) for students and faculty members of schools, colleges, and other institutions in order to instil the concepts and benefits of standardisation in the minds of young people.

World Standards Day: On the 14th of October, BIS commemorates World Standards Day to honour the joint efforts of thousands of professionals across the world who establish voluntary technical agreements that are published as International or National Standards.

Public Grievances: Consumer complaints about BIS-certified products are assessed and monitored on a regular basis for possible resolution.

Public Relations: The BIS PR campaign aims to raise awareness of various BIS operations within its target audience, which includes industry and the general public, particularly those connected to standardisation, certification of goods and services, and gold jewellery hallmarking.

Watch and Ward: The Creation

After delving into the nitty-gritty of the proposed concept, the Committee concluded that a Security service should be established immediately to secure and monitor the Parliament House's inner precincts and to keep a vigil/watch on unlawful activity within Parliament. The Committee wisely chose the name "WATCH AND WARD" for the organisation.

The name of the Legislative Assembly Department (LAD) remained the same until 26 January 1950, when it was changed to 'PARLIAMENT SECRETARIAT' with the entry into force of the Constitution of India and the establishment of a Provisional Parliament. With the formation of two independent Houses in 1952, the House of the People's Secretariat was renamed the Parliament Secretariat, while the Council of States' Secretariat was renamed the Council of States Secretariat. In 1954, their titles were altered to 'LokSabha Secretariat' and 'Rajya Sabha Secretariat,' respectively, to conform to the Hindi nomenclature of the Houses.

These two secretariats began operating as separate bodies under the ultimate leadership and authority of the respective chambers' Chairman/ Speaker. Throughout all of the Constitutional changes that the Parliament witnessed, the Watch and Ward service remained to provide protection. For administrative purposes, each House was given its own Secretariat, and a separate location was set aside for the newly formed Council of States/ Rajya Sabha Secretariat.

Watch and Ward: The Multifaceted Growth

With the passage of time, Watch and Ward specialised on the identification of Members of Parliament and high-ranking officials. Their services began to be requisitioned outside the Parliament House complex for national festivities such as Rajpath's Republic Day celebrations, Red Fort's Independence Day celebrations, 'At Home' functions, and Rashtrapati Bhavan's swearing-in ceremonies, among others. In view of the ever-changing security circumstances and threat perception, the security arrangements in Parliament were further enhanced.

As National and International Parliamentary Conferences began to meet, the responsibilities of Watch and Ward grew exponentially, including receiving and seeing off National and International delegates at the airport, looking after their lodging and boarding at hotels, security arrangements at the hotels, and accompanying them to places of sightseeing, in addition to performing duties at the conference venue.

Watch and Ward: The Unparalleled

The Watch and Ward department has evolved into an unrivalled organisation that performs extremely sensitive security activities within its constraints. Even at the danger of their life, the unarmed Watch and Ward staff undertakes security tasks for the historical and prestigious Parliament House edifice, its members, and the VVIPs.

CHAPTER VIII

Marketing-Demand, Supply, Supply Forecasting, Branding, Packaging, Warranty

Introduction

Marketing

Marketing refers to the activities that a company engages in to promote the purchase or sale of a product or service. Advertising, selling, and delivering products to consumers or other businesses is all part of marketing. Affiliates do some marketing on a company's behalf.

Professionals in a corporation's marketing and promotion departments use advertising to capture the attention of key potential audiences. Promotions are aimed at specific demographics and may include celebrity endorsements, memorable phrases or slogans, memorable packaging or graphic designs, and overall media exposure.

Marketing as a discipline encompasses all of the actions that a company takes to attract and retain customers. Networking with potential or past clients is also a part of the job, and may include writing thank you emails, playing golf with prospective clients, promptly returning phone calls and emails, and meeting with clients for coffee or a meal.

Marketing, at its most basic, seeks to match a company's products and services to customers who want access to those products. Ultimately, matching products to customers ensures profitability.

The Four Ps of marketing are product, price, place, and promotion. The Four Ps constitute the essential mix required by a company to market a product or service.

The Importance of Marketing in today's World

While the brain of a business is the finance department, body the product offered, the heart is the marketing department of the business which pumps oxygen and the necessary nutrients to every other body part. Unlike the old times, marketing no more deals only in the communication of the product to the consumers. The activity is now found in every aspect of the business. One should not turn a blind eye to the importance of marketing as marketing fuels both the external and internal.

Today, large and small-scale, global and local, innovative and traditional, public and private, everyone is competing for the same market. Companies have realized the power of holistic approach to marketing to create and maintain a desirable demand, reputation, and competition. The role of marketing is too diverse to be summarised in one small article. Nevertheless, we've come up with few arguments to state the importance of marketing in today's world. l activities of the business today.

Creating a Brand

According to Stephen King of the WPP Group:

"A product is something that is made in a factory a brand is something that is bought by a customer. A product can be copied by a competitor, a brand is unique. A product can be quickly outdated, a successful brand is timeless"

The brand is the company's most valuable asset and the sole responsibility to create a brand lies on the shoulder of the marketing department of the organization. The market is full of similar products and the only thing which makes the company stand out is its brand. Today, Brand is not just a combination of name, symbol, and design, it is the business-consumer relationship, the consumers' perception, and the consumers' opinion about the company and its products. Along with the symbolic value, a brand also carries an awareness value which eventually leads to brand loyalty and more sales if taken care of properly.

Product Development

One of the most important aspects of product development is to search for a perfect market for the product, get consumer insights, and develop a perfect proposition to make it stand out of the rest. The 4p's of marketing play a huge role in the product development.

Communication

Competition is everywhere and sometimes it's only the good communication strategy which makes the brand stands out of the rest. New communication avenues like internet, smart devices, and social media, have opened the doors to new and more targeted communication strategies which eventually lead to more conversions.

In this competitive environment, a product without communication is a dead product. Communication infuses life in it and triggers sales.

Building Relationships

A relationship is built on trust, understanding, and pride. Marketing plays a very significant role in building a relationship between the customers and the organization. It works along with the product team to deliver what's promised at the time of and after the sale has taken place. The relationship, once built, makes the customers more brand loyal and gives them the confidence to repeat sales and buy more products under the same brand. The relationship further narrows down the marketing funnel by removing the top two stages (awareness & interest) and making the business activities more fruitful.

Maintaining The Company's Reputation

The success and the life-span of the company are positively correlated to the company's reputation which usually is correlated to the brand equity of the business. A majority of the activities of the marketers are directed towards building the brand equity of the business.

Company's reputation is built when it successfully fulfils the expectations of its customers, when it acts like a responsible member of the society, and when the customers feel proud of using its products. Marketers by using effective communication, CSR, PR, and branding strategies, make sure that the company's reputation is maintained.

Tackling the Competition

Competition has reached an all-time high to a point where the only difference in most of the cases is not a product feature but how it is communicated to the user. New communication avenues are being explored along with new markets. Marketing plays a vital role in tackling the competition by not only deciding which feature will sell but also planning strategies on how to portray it better than the other players.

Customers are more informed as they were a few years ago. Deception and short-term sales strategies not only backfire on the product but also the brand. This has led to more burden on the shoulders of the marketers.

Demand

Demand is an economic principle referring to a consumer's desire to purchase goods and services and willingness to pay a price for a specific good or service. Holding all other factors constant, an increase in the price of a good or service will decrease the quantity demanded, and vice versa. Market demand is the total quantity demanded across all consumers in a market for a given good. Aggregate demand is the total demand for all goods and services in an economy. Multiple stocking strategies are often required to handle demand.

Demand is closely related to supply. While consumers try to pay the lowest prices they can for goods and services, suppliers try to maximize profits. If suppliers charge too much, the quantity demanded drops and suppliers do not sell enough product to earn sufficient profits. If suppliers charge too little, the quantity demanded increases but lower prices may not cover suppliers' costs or allow for profits. Some factors affecting demand include the appeal of a good or service, the availability of competing goods, the availability of financing, and the perceived availability of a good or service.

Law Demand : The law of demand is one of the most fundamental concepts in economics. It works with the law of supply to explain how market economies allocate resources and determine the prices of goods and services that we observe in everyday transactions.

The law of demand states that quantity purchased varies inversely with price. In other words, the higher the price, the lower the quantity demanded. This occurs because of diminishing marginal utility. That is, consumers use the first units of an economic good they purchase to serve their most urgent needs first, and use each additional unit of the good to serve successively lower-valued ends.

Demand Curve : The demand curve is a graphical representation of the relationship between the price of a good or service and the quantity demanded for a given period of time. In a typical representation, the price will appear on the left vertical axis, the quantity demanded on the horizontal axis.

Supply

Supply is the willingness and ability of producers to create goods and services to take them to market. Supply is positively related to price given that at higher prices there is an incentive to supply more as higher prices may generate increased revenue and profits.

Supply is the amount of a resource that firms, producers, labourers, providers of financial assets, or other economic agents are willing and able to provide to the marketplace or directly to another agent in the marketplace. Supply can be in currency, time, raw materials, or any other scarce or valuable object that can be provided to another agent. This is often fairly abstract. For example in the case of time, supply is not transferred to one agent from another, but one agent may offer some other resource in exchange for the first spending time doing something. Supply is often plotted graphically as a supply curve, with the quantity provided (the dependent variable) plotted horizontally and the price (the independent variable) plotted vertically.

In the goods market, supply is the amount of a product per unit of time that producers are willing to sell at various given prices when all other factors are held constant. In the labour market, the supply of labour is the amount of time per week, month, or year that individuals are willing to spend working, as a function of the wage rate.

Factors affecting supply

Innumerable factors and circumstances could affect a seller's willingness or ability to produce and sell a good. Some of the more common factors are:

Good's own price: The basic supply relationship is between the price of a good and the quantity supplied. Although there is no "Law of Supply", generally, the relationship is positive, meaning that an increase in price will induce an increase in the quantity supplied

Prices of related goods: For purposes of supply analysis related goods refer to goods example, Spam is made from pork shoulders and ham. Both are derived from pigs. Therefore, pigs would be considered a related good to Spam. In this case the relationship would be negative or inverse. If the price of pigs goes up the supply of Spam would decrease (supply curve shifts left) because the cost of production would have increased. A related good may also be a good that can be produced with the firm's existing factors of production. For example, suppose that a firm produces leather belts, and that the firm's managers learn that leather pouches for smartphones are more profitable than belts. The firm might reduce its production of belts and begin production of cell phone pouches based on this information. Finally, a change in the price of a joint product will affect supply. For example, beef products and leather are joint products. If a company runs both a beef processing operation and a tannery an increase in the price of steaks would mean that more cattle are processed which would increase the supply of leather.

Conditions of production: The most significant factor here is the state of technology. If there is a technological advancement in one good's production, the supply increases. Other variables may also affect production conditions. For instance, for agricultural goods, weather is crucial for it may affect the production outputs. Economies of scale can also affect conditions of production.

Expectations: Sellers' concern for future market conditions can directly affect supply. If the seller believes that the demand for his product will sharply increase in the foreseeable future the firm owner may immediately increase production in anticipation of future price increases. The supply curve would shift out.

Price of inputs: Inputs include land, labor, energy and raw materials.] If the price of inputs increases the supply curve will shift left as sellers are less willing or able to sell goods at any given price. For example, if the price of electricity increased a seller may reduce his supply of his product because of the increased costs of production. Fixed inputs can affect the price of inputs, and the scale of production can affect how much the fixed costs translate into the end price of the good.

Number of suppliers: The market supply curve is the horizontal summation of the individual supply curves. As more firms enter the industry, the market supply curve will shift out, driving down prices.

Government policies and regulations: government intervention can have a significant effect on supply. Government intervention can take many forms including environmental and health regulations, hour and wage laws, taxes, electrical and natural gas rates and zoning and land use regulations.

Supply curve: The supply curve is a graphic representation of the correlation between the cost of a good or service and the quantity supplied for a given period. In a typical illustration, the price will appear on the left vertical axis, while the quantity supplied will appear on the horizontal axis.

Theory of Demand and Supply

We know that a market is an arrangement that enables buyers and sellers to get information and do business with each other. A competitive market is a market that has many buyers and many sellers so no single buyer or seller can influence the price. The money price of a good is the amount of money needed to buy it. The relative price of a good—the ratio of its money price to the money price of the next best alternative good—is its opportunity cost.

The market is governed by the law of demand. First, let us define what we mean by demand in terms of the market:

Demand for commodity implies (i) the desire to acquire it, (ii) willingness to pay for it, (iii) ability to pay for it. The Law of demand states that:

The relationship between Price and quantity demanded is an economic law. The quantity of a good demanded per period relates inversely to its price, other things constant.

The law of demand results from (i) Substitution effect, (ii) Income effect.

Browse more Topics under Economics and Governance

- Comptroller and Auditor General of India
- Defense
- Summits

- Constituency and Ministry of Cabinet Ministers
- Ministers and Portfolio
- Finance Commission

Substitution Effect

When the relative price (opportunity cost) of a good or service rises, people seek substitutes for it, so the quantity demanded of the good or service decreases.

Income Effect

When the price of a good or service rises relative to income, people cannot afford all the things they previously bought, so the quantity demanded of the good or service decreases.

Demand Curve and Demand Schedule

The term demand refers to the entire relationship between the price of the good and quantity demanded of the good.

A demand curve shows the relationship between the quantity demanded of a good and its price when all other influences on consumers' planned purchases remain the same.

An exception to Law of Demand: Giffen Goods

A Giffen good is one which people paradoxically consume more of as the price rises, violating the law of demand. For example, during the Irish Potato Famine of the 19th century, potatoes were considered a Giffen good. Potatoes were the largest staple in the Irish diet, so as the price rose it had a large impact on income.

People responded by cutting out on luxury goods such as meat and vegetables, and instead bought more potatoes. Therefore, as the price of potatoes increased, so did the demand.

Demand Schedule and Demand Curve

The demand schedule is a table that shows the relationship between the price of the good and the quantity demanded.

The demand curve is a graph of the relationship between the price of a good and the quantity demanded.

Types of Demand

- **Individual Demand**

The quantity of a commodity an individual is willing and able to purchase at a particular price, during a specific time period, given his/her money income, his/her taste, and prices of other commodities, such as substitutes and complements, is referred to as the individual demand for the commodity.

- **Market Demand**

The total quantity which all the consumers of the commodity are willing and able to purchase at a given price per time unit, given their money incomes, their tastes, and prices of other commodities, is referred to as the market demand for the commodity.

- **Autonomous Demand**

An autonomous demand or direct demand for a commodity is one that arises on its own out of a natural desire to consume or possess a commodity. This type of demand is independent of the demand for other commodities.

- **Durable Demand**

Durable goods are those goods for which the total utility or usefulness is not exhaustible in the short-run use. Such goods can be used repeatedly over a period of time.

- **Non-Durable Demand**

The demand for non-durable goods depends largely on their current prices, consumers' income, and fashion. It is also subject to frequent changes.

Short-Term and Long-Term Demand

Short-term demand refers to the demand for goods over a short period.

The long-term demand refers to the demand which exists over a long period of time.

Factors Influencing Demand

Following are the main factors that influence the demand of an object:

- Price of good or service (P)
- Incomes of consumers (M)
- Prices of related goods & services (PR)

- Taste patterns of the consumer (T)
- Expected future price of the product (Pe)
- Number of consumers in a market (N)

Market Demand

Market demand is the sum of all individual demands at each possible price. Graphically, individual demand curves are summed horizontally to obtain the market demand curve.

Supply

If a firm supplies a good or service, then the firm:

1. Has the resources and the technology to produce it,
2. Can profit from producing it, and
3. Has made a definite plan to produce and sell it.

Resources and technology determine what it is possible to produce. Supply reflects a decision about which technologically feasible items to produce. The quantity supplied of a good or service is the amount that producers plan to sell during a given time period at a particular price.

The Law of Supply

The law of supply states:

Other things remaining the same, the higher the price of a good, the greater is the quantity supplied; and the lower the price of a good, the smaller is the quantity supplied.

The law of supply results from the general tendency for the marginal cost of producing a good or service to increase as the quantity produced increases. Producers are willing to supply a good only if they can at least cover their marginal cost of production.

Supply Curve and Supply Schedule

The term supply refers to the entire relationship between the quantity supplied and the price of a good. The supply curve shows the relationship between the quantity supplied of a good and its price when all other influences on producers' planned sales remain the same.

A supply curve is also a minimum-supply-price curve. As the quantity produced increases, marginal cost increases. The lowest price at which someone is willing to sell an additional unit rises.

A Change in Supply

The six main factors that change the supply of a good are:

a. The prices of factors of production

b. The prices of related goods produced

c. Expected future prices
d. The number of supplier's
e. Technology
f. State of nature

Market Equilibrium

Equilibrium is a situation in which opposing forces balance each other. Equilibrium in a market occurs when the price balances the plans of buyers and sellers.

The equilibrium price is the price at which the quantity demanded equals the quantity supplied. The equilibrium quantity is the quantity bought and sold at the equilibrium price.

The price regulates buying and selling plans.

Price adjusts when plans don't match.

Demand and Supply Forecasting:

Demand Forecasting:

Demand forecasting is a quantitative aspect of human resource planning. It is the process of estimating the future requirement of human resources of all kinds and types of the organisation.

Methods of Demand Forecasting:

There are three major methods of demand forecasting. They are as follows.

(1) Executive Judgment:

The executive or Managerial Judgment method is the most suitable for smaller enterprises because they do not afford to have work-study technique. Under this method the executives sit together and determine the future manpower requirements of the enterprise and submit the proposal to the top management for approval. This approach is known as the 'bottom up' approach.

(2) Work Load Forecasting:

It is also known as work load analysis. Under this method the stock of workload and the continuity of operations are determined. Accordingly the labour requirement is determined. The workload becomes the base for workforce analysis for the forthcoming years. Here due consideration is given to absenteeism and labour turnover. This method is also known as work study technique. Here working capacity of each employee is calculated in terms of man-hours. Man-hours required for each unit is calculated and then number of required employees is calculated.

(3) Statistical Techniques:

Long range demand forecasting for human resources is more responsive to statistical and mathematical techniques. With the help of computers any data is rapidly analyzed.

Supply Forecasting:

Supply forecasting means to make an estimation of supply of human resources taking into consideration the analysis of current human resources inventory and future availability.

Sources of Supply:

Estimation of supply of human resources depends upon internal and external sources.

Internal Factors:

Internal source of supply of human resources include the output from established training programme for employees and management development programmes for executives and the existing reservoirs of skills, potentials, creative abilities of the organisation.

External Factors:

External factors can be grouped into local and national factors.

(1) Population densities within the reach of enterprise.

(2) Current and future wage and salary structure from other employers.

(3) Local unemployment level.

(4) Availability of employees on part time, temporary and casual basis.

Forecasting supply includes figuring out what faculty will be accessible. The two sources are inward and outer: individuals previously utilized by the firm and those external the association. Variables supervisors ordinarily consider when forecasting the supply of workforce incorporate advancing representatives from inside the association; recognizing workers willing and ready to prepare; accessibility of required ability in nearby, provincial, and public work markets; rivalry for ability inside the field; populace patterns (like the development of families in the United States from Northeast toward the Southwest); school and college enlistment patterns in the required field.

Interior wellsprings of workers to fill projected opportunities should check. This encourages by the utilization of the human asset review or the orderly stock of the capabilities of existing staff. A human asset review is just an authoritative outline of a unit or whole association with all positions (generally managerial) show and key regarding the "promo ability" of every job occupant.

6 best Key relationship or difference Between Demand Forecasting Planning and Supply Forecasting Planning:

Forthcoming focuses will disclose to you the relationship or difference between demand and supply forecasting planning:

1. Demand is the ability and paying limit of a purchaser at a particular cost. Then again, Supply is the amount offered by the makers to their clients at a particular cost.
2. While the demand bend is descending to one side, the supply bend is upward to one side. And so the demand bend is a negative slant though the supply bend is a positive slant.
3. Demand has a roundabout relationship with the cost for example as the cost expands, the amount demanded diminishes, and it the other way around. Then again, the supply has an immediate relationship with cost as in when the cost expands, the amount provided increments, and the other way around
4. While demand is a pointer of clients or purchasers, supply addresses the firm or makers of the item.
5. Demand for an item affects by five variables – Taste and Preference, Number of Consumers, Price of Related Goods, Income, Consumer Expectations. Conversely, Supply for the item is subject to the Price of the Resources and different data sources, Number of Producers, Technology, Taxes and Subsidies, Consumer Expectations.
6. At the point when the demand increments however supply stays steady, it prompts deficiency yet when the demand diminishes and the supply is consistent prompts excess. As against, when the supply increments yet demand stays consistent, it prompts excess however when the supply diminishes and the demand is steady it brings about deficiency.

Product Pricing:

Pricing is something that only seldom gets its due importance. Many businesses, esp. start-ups, possibly go to the nth depth of the product design, however, will mostly think of the price when the product is either about to be launched in the market, or after it starts getting beaten in the market post-launch. Even then, only rarely do they think of pricing strategically. Many times, given limited resources, it's just Cost-Plus. Sometimes, competition pricing clouts the decision. Rarely, the value generated by the product becomes the foundation for the pricing.

There are three components to the overall pricing strategy:

1. Choice of a Pricing Principle: Cost-Plus, Competitive, Value-Based
2. Choice of a Price Positioning: Market Skimming, Neutral, Penetration
3. Choice of a Pricing Structure: Unit Pricing, Tiered Pricing, Bundled Pricing, Subscriptions etc.

"To meet the demands of industrial customers seeking value, the seller must understand value from the buyer's point of view and use that information in determining price."

Branding and Packaging

Branding:

Branding is the process of stamping a product with some identifying mark or name or a combination of both. It means giving a separate and unique identification to the product which will distinct it in the market.

What does Branding Do?

A branding has a lot of functions to perform. These are as follows:

Publicity: The most important benefit of establishing a brand is that it helps in the publicity of the product. Once the product is established under the brand, it can be easily advertised and people have a better reliability of the brand. People remember it for a long period of time.

Wide Market: The branding helps in the placement of the product over a large number of markets. It gets easy for a brand to explore other markets as well for their products. The larger or wider the market a brand has, the more it will be able to sell its products.

Distinctiveness: A brand helps in creating a separate image in front of the people. The people are able to easily differentiate between the branded products and the other products. This distinctiveness helps the business to grow all the more and increase its This helps in the easy placement of the product in the market.

Protection of Goods: A brand helps in the protection of the goods. Generally, the branded products are packed in suitable containers or wrappers which provide protection to the goods against heat and moisture and facilitate convenient handling.

Consumer Protection: The prices of branded products are fixed by the manufacturers and are printed on the packages. This protects the interest of the consumers because the retailer cannot charge more than the printed prices. The prices of the branded goods remain the same at different places over a considerable period of time.

Consumer Loyalty: Branding ensures a better quality at competitive prices. Branded products are available in all parts of the country at uniform prices. This tends to create brand loyalty on the part of the customer.

What are the benefits of Branding?

Ensures Quality: Branding ensures a particular level of quality of the product. Thus the customer can buy branded goods with confidence about their quality.

Product Differentiation: Branding helps the customers in identifying the goods among other products easily due to its distinctiveness. Branding facilitates the repeat purchase of the products.

Psychological Satisfaction: Consumer buying differentiated brands feels satisfied not only with the physical product or service but also psychologically. Buying some branded product over which they can rely on, brings psychological satisfaction to them.

Easy Shopping: Branding makes shopping easier because the consumer knows what product to buy. For example, if a person wants to buy Sony Television, he can go to Sony authorized dealer and by the model of his choice.

Status Symbol: Some brands are advertised heavily and they create some sort of status symbol among the consumer groups.

Uniform Price: The branded products are always charged at a uniform price all over the areas.

Packaging:

Packaging involves designing and producing of container or wrapper for a product in order to prepare the goods for transport, sale and usage. There is a difference between packing and packaging. Packing refers to the covering of goods with a wrapper or putting the goods in some container; whereas packaging is a part of product planning intended to satisfy the needs of customers.

There are three levels of packaging:

1. **Primary Package:** It refers to the immediate container or package of a product. It remains with the product until it is used. For example, toothpaste tube, matchbox Primary package is essential to hold the core product.
2. **Secondary Package:** It is an additional package that gives additional protection to the product. Example: The card paper box package of the

toothpaste tube is a secondary package.

3. **Shipping or Transport Package:** The shipping package is the bulk packaging necessary to store, identify and ship the product. IT holds the secondary packages for storing and shipments. Such packaging gives protection to the secondary packaging and facilitated transportation.

Functions of Packaging:

1. **Protection of the product:** The basic function of the packaging is to protect the product from any breakage or damage due to mishandling, extremes of temperature, contamination with extra elements such as dirt and chemical elements, absorption of moisture or odor, loss of liquid or vapor or any pilferage.
2. **Appeal to the customer:** Package I an important marketing tool particularly for consumer products such as cosmetics, chocolates, toffees etc. A package reforms the self- selling tasks. It I often referred to as the silent seller.
3. **Easy handling:** Packaged goods are very easy to handle. Handling instructions can also be mentioned on the package to ensure safe handling of the goods.
4. **Publicity to the product:** Packaging gives individuality to the product and these acts as a device of publicity. Manufacturers choose attractive packaging designs so as to attract the customers to buy the product.
5. **Cost-effective:** A package costs the manufacturer. The cost of the package should not alarmingly increase
6. **Preventing Adulteration:** Packaging is also necessary to prevent adulteration of goods by the unscrupulous traders. For instance, Oils, cheese etc. can be adulterated easily and thus require proper packaging.
7. **Convenience:** A good design of the package would provide many advantages convenient to stock, display. Not waste shelf space, retails it looks during shelf display and is easy to dispose of- off. Thus, standardization of the packages provides great convenience to the manufacturers, resellers and the consumers.

Sales Promotion:

Sales promotion is a set of marketing technologies aimed to stimulate the demand in particular products and increase brand awareness. Limited in time, it creates a feeling of time-sensitiveness, generates new leads, and keeps existing customers engaged.

Benefits of sales promotion :

- It helps to generate new leads
- Allows re-engaging with your existing audience
- Skyrockets revenue
- Increases brand awareness.

1. It helps to generate new leads. Sales promotion can boost your product image since it encourages sharing information about it within social groups related to your business. If you sell training football shoes, people keen on playing football will share the message.
2. Allows re-engaging with your existing audience. Once a person subscribed to a brand's email newsletter, they will receive regular sales promotions. It is a way to keep the audience engaged and maintain a close connection with the company, which is crucial for building loyality.
3. Skyrockets revenue. Sales promotions help companies to increase the number of sold goods, even though they need to lower the price to achieve that goal. Of course, merely reducing the price is not enough, people should need your product, while the discount is only another reason to make a purchase.
4. Increases brand awareness. Sales promotion is a way to make a name for your brand because people are more likely to talk about a company that proposes benefits and saves their money. That's what sales promotion does.

Sales Promotion Ideas

- Give an adequate range of discounts
- Target sales promotion to the right people
- Take advantage of the shopping holidays
- Create a sense of urgency
- Develop a loyalty program
- Use sales promotion to generate leads
- Offer free shipping.

Advertising

Advertising is a marketing communication that employs an openly sponsored, non-personal message to promote or sell a product, service or idea. Sponsors of advertising are typically businesses wishing to promote their products or services. Advertising is differentiated from public relations in that an advertiser pays for and has control over the message. It differs from personal selling in that the message is non-personal, i.e., not directed to a particular individual. Advertising is communicated through various mass media, including traditional media such as newspapers, magazines, television, radio or direct mail; and new media such as search results, blogs, social media, websites or text messages. The actual presentation of the message in a medium is referred to as an advertisement: advert or ad for short.

Commercial ads often seek to generate increased consumption of their products or services through "branding ", which associates a product name or image with certain qualities in the minds of consumers. On the other hand, ads that intend to elicit an immediate sale are known as direct response advertising. Non-commercial entities that advertise more than consumer products or services include political parties, interest groups, religious organizations and governmental agencies. Non-profit organizations may use free modes of persuasion, such as a public service announcement. . Advertising may also help to reassure employees or shareholders that a company is viable or successful.

Publicity

In marketing, publicity is the public visibility or awareness for any product, service or organization (company, charity, etc.). It may also refer to the movement of information from its source to the general public, often (but not always) via the media. The subjects of publicity include people of public interest, goods and services, organizations, and works of art or entertainment.

A publicist is someone that carries out publicity, while public relations (PR) is the strategic management function that helps an organization establish and maintain communication with the public. This can be done internally, without the use of popular media. From a marketing perspective, publicity is one component of promotion and marketing. The other elements of the promotional mix are advertising, sales promotion, direct marketing and personal selling.

Organizations will sometimes organize events designed to attract media coverage, and subsequently, provide positive publicity; these events are known as publicity stunts.

Negative Publicity:

Publicity can also create a negative effect for those being publicized. One of the most important factors in relation to influencing a consumer's buying decision is how a company, brand, or individual deals with negative publicity. Negative publicity may result in major loss of revenue or market shares within a business. It can also play a part in damaging a consumer's perception of a brand or its products. Negative publicity's high credibility and greater influence compared to other company-controlled communications play a part in the potential damage it may have on a corporate image. Crises involved with an organization may also result in negative publicity.

While publicity may be a component of your marketing strategy, it's different from marketing because there is no message beyond letting an audience know that the product or service in question exists.

Marketing involves communicating specific benefits and emotions to potential customers to persuade them to make a purchase. Publicity is designed to make a person, product, or brand more visible.

Marketing is almost always directed at a business's target audience. Publicity typically targets a broader audience.

Key Takeaways

Publicity is media attention for your product, service, or business. It can include traditional news sources, like news shows and newspapers, and new media, like podcasts, blogs, and websites.

Publicity raises awareness of your business, and can often be generated for free.

Publicity is different from marketing; it's general and doesn't carry a specific message. Marketing is promoting your product or service.

You can generate publicity through social media, product placements, strategic partnerships, and promotional swag.

Warranty and After-Sale Service

Warranty

In contract law, a warranty is a promise which is not a condition of the contract or an innominate it is a term "not going to the root of the contract and which only entitles the innocent party to damages if it is breached: i.e. the warranty is not true or the defaulting party does not perform the contract in accordance with the terms of the warranty. A warranty is not a guarantee. It is a mere promise. It may be enforced if it is breached by an award for the legal remedy of damages.

A warranty is a term of a contract. Depending on the terms of the contract, a product warranty may cover a product such that a manufacturer provides a warranty to a consumer with which the manufacturer has no direct contractual relationship.

A warranty may be express or implied. An express warranty is expressly stated (typically, written); whether or not a term will be implied into a contract depends on the particular contract law of the country in question. Warranties may also state that a particular fact is true at one point in time or that the fact will continue into the future (a "continuing warranty")

Sales of Good

Warranties provided in the sale of goods (tangible products) vary according to jurisdiction, but commonly new goods are sold with implied warranty that the goods are as advertised. Used products, however, may be sold "as is" with no warranties. Each country, however, defines its own parameters with regard to implied conditions or implied warranties. This is because each country (a country as defined by international civil law) has its own system of contract law with its own set of rules. Said rules are largely standardised; i.e., the concepts of offer acceptance, consideration, capacity to contract and intention to create legal relations. are the five elements to create a legally binding contract in the United States (all 50 states), England and Wales, Scotland and Northern Ireland, each of the seven states of Australia, and all other common law countries. Countries with civil law, however, recognise legally binding contracts which are not supported by consideration.

In the United States, various laws apply, including provisions in the uniform commercial code which provide for implied warranties. However, these implied warranties were often limited by disclaimers In 1975 Magnuson-moss warranty act was passed to strengthen warranties on consumer goods. Among other things, under the law implied warranties cannot be disclaimed if an express warranty is offered, and attorney fees may be recovered. In some states, statutory warranties are required on new home construction, and "lemon laws" apply to motor vehicles.

Extended Warranty

In addition to standard warranties on new items, third parties or manufacturers may sell or offer extended warranties (also called service contracts). These extend the warranty for a further length of time. However, these warranties have terms and conditions which may not match the original terms and conditions. For example, these may not cover anything other than mechanical failure from normal usage. Exclusions may include commercial use, "acts of God", owner abuse, and malicious destruction. They may also exclude parts that normally wear out such as tires and lubrication on a vehicle.

These types of warranties are provided for various products, but automobiles and electronics are common examples. Warranties that are sold through retailers such as best buys may include a significant commission for the retailer as a result of reverse competition. For instance, an auto warranty from a car dealership may be subcontracted and vehicle repairs may be at a lower rate which could compromise the quality of service. At the time of repair, out-of-pocket expenses may be charged for unexpected services provided outside of the warranty terms or uncovered parts.

After Sales Services

After-sales service refers to all the things you do for the care and feeding of your valued customers after they buy your product. This type of customer aftercare is important for any business, but especially for small businesses where every client counts.

It's not enough to say "Thanks" or "Let's keep in touch" after a sale is complete. Long-term success is built on real and lasting customer relationships.

Sit back while Natalie explains precisely what is after-sales service, and why it's important for your small business

Top-quality after-sales service is good for you because it's good for your customer. When you help them get the most out of your product or service, they're naturally happier with it. That makes them more likely to order again and to tell the world, too.

To put it another way: the more you wow your customers, the more they're likely to wow you right back with their loyalty and enthusiasm. They'll become the brand ambassadors, reviewers, and trusted voices who'll give you great reviews, sing your praises on social media and give you honest feedback on new products and features.

Let's look at some after-sales support examples that will keep customers happy while driving new business. Or start a demo and learn how keep can help you improve your customer aftercare.

After-sales is the provision of services, support and spare parts after making an initial sale. This often occurs in the provision of complex machinery which requires regular maintenance such as motor vehicle.

Difference between Warranty and Guarantee

Warranty

The guarantee is a sort of commitment made by the manufacturer to the purchaser of goods, whereas a Warranty is an assurance given to the buyer by the manufacturer of the goods.

Guarantee

The guarantee covers product, service, persons and consumer satisfaction while warranty covers products only. The guarantee is free of cost.

Product Development

Product development, also called New Product Development (NPD), is a series of steps that includes the conceptualization, design, development and marketing of newly created or newly rebranded goods or services. The objective of product development is to cultivate, maintain and increase a company's market share by satisfying a consumer demand. Not every product will appeal to every customer or client base, so defining the target market for a product is a critical component that must take place early in the product development process. Quantitative market research should be conducted at all phases of the design process, including before the product or service is conceived, while the product is being designed and after the product has been launched.

Product development is a specialized activity. It is done to improve the existing product or to introduce a new product in the market. It is also done to improve the earlier features or techniques or systems. Generally, it means a new product development. New-product development means introducing a brand-new product in the market. It means to add a fresh product to an existing line of products. Normally, a company starts with one or two products. However, after some time it has few more products in its line (say from 15 to 20). This is possible only because of new-product development. Refer the following diagram to know the basic meaning of product development.

Product development takes place, works or functions as under:

Creation of an entirely new product or upgrading an existing product by exploring all possibilities and outcomes.

Innovation of a new or an existing product to deliver better and enhanced services to end-users.Continuous improvement of a new product or enhancing an existing product by giving preference to satisfy the demand of end-users.Enhancing the utility of a new product or upgrading features of an existing product, for personal and/or commercial use, to expand the defined goal.

Product Development Process

Product development is an engineering process to convert product idea into finished products. It's a series of steps that include the product concept, structure, material, manufacturing, and marketing. Developing a new product can capture a new business opportunity as well as expanding market shares, it's quite important for all of companies, especially for startups. Even though product development steps might vary a lot from different business size and different project management style, however most projects follow the **main steps in the product design and development process as below:**

1. **Idea generation** – brainstorming and coming up with innovative new ideas. See generating ideas for new products and services.
2. **Idea evaluation** - filtering out any ideas not worth taking forward. See screening new product or service idea.
3. **Concept definition** - considering specifications such as technical feasibility, product design and market potential. See researching new product and service ideas.
4. **Strategic analysis** - ensuring your ideas fit into your business'strategic plans and determining the demand, the costs and the profit margin.
5. **Product development and testing** - creating a prototype product or pilot service. See concept development and testing.
6. **Market testing** - modifying the product or service according to customer, manufacturer and support organisations' feedback. This involves deciding the best timing and process for piloting your new product or service. See how to test the market.
7. **Commercialization** – determining the pricing for your product or service and finalising marketing plans. See pricing your proposed service or product.
8. **Product launch** – a detailed launch plan can help ensure a smooth introduction to market.

Product improvement

It is aimed at bringing about significant changes with the purpose of getting new clients, retaining existing users, and recapturing lost customers. In fact, there are two ways of improving products: adding fresh features and upgrading existing ones.

New specs and updates make a current product more advanced. Such a solution enhances the value proposition and expands the target audience base. Plus, it drives value for existing customers, diminishes churn rate, and contributes to building brand loyalty.

Bringing already existing features up to date is another story. You have three different opportunities here:

Intentional improvements: simply make a product better when you know why people use it and what value they see in it;

Regular improvements: tweak features so that customers avail of a product more often and gain real benefits;

Introductory improvements: change features you think will make the lives of new clients much easier.

Salesmanship

The term salesmanship is mainly used for the sale of goods at a personal level.

Definition of salesmanship

Salesmanship can be defined as the ability of a person to sell a product or service to a customer by removing their ignorance and doubtfulness about the product in such a way that both the buyer as well as the seller gets to benefit from the deal.

The contemporary idea of salesmanship is quite different from the older concept of salesmanship. In the ancient times, the salesperson used to carry goods with him and showed it to the customers to sell them, or he used to give the samples of products to prospective customers and wait for their order.

That means, at that time, the power was in the hands of customers. But the modern concept of salesmanship has changed. Now, salespersons meet the prospective customers and create the need for the product. They make their potential customers believe that how much that product is crucial for them, and by selling the product to them, they satisfy the needs of their customers.

What Is a Tender?

A tender is an invitation to bid for a project or accept a formal offer such as a takeover bid. Tendering usually refers to the process whereby governments and financial institutions invite bids for large projects that must be submitted within a finite deadline. The term also refers to the process whereby shareholders submit their shares or securities in response to a takeover offer.

Some points on Tender

Tender usually refers to the process whereby governments and financial institutions invite bids for large projects that must be submitted within a finite deadline.

A tender offer is a public solicitation to all shareholders requesting that they tender their stock for sale at a specific price during a certain time.

A request for tender (RFT) is a formal and structured invitation to suppliers to submit competitive bids to supply raw materials, products, or services.

The term tender also refers to the process whereby shareholders submit their shares or securities in response to a takeover offer.

Contracts

What is a Contract?

As usual in the law, the legal definition of "contract" is formalistic. The Restatement says:

"A contract is a promise or a set of promises for the breach of which the law gives a remedy, or the performance of which the law in some way recognizes as a duty."

Similarly, the Uniform Commercial Code says:

"Contract means the total legal obligation which results from the parties' agreement as affected by this Act and any other applicable rules of law."

A short-hand definition is: "***A contract is a legally enforceable promise".***

Conditions for a Contract

In every contract an offer makes an offer to enter into a contract with an offeree. The offer or offers to do something in particular (or to refrain from doing something in particular), and if the offeree accepts this offer, a contract is created.

As you can also see, both offer and acceptance must meet certain conditions.

A contract is legally enforceable: if one party fails to do what he or she has promised to do, the other can ask the courts to enforce the agreement or award damages for injury sustained because the contract has been breached—because a promise made under the contract hasn't been kept or an act hasn't been performed. A contract, however, can be enforced only if it meets four requirements:

Agreement: The parties must have reached a mutual agreement. The offer or must have made an offer, and the offeree must have replied with an acceptance.

Consideration: Each promise must be made in return for the performance of a legally sufficient act or promise. If one party isn't required to exchange something of legal value (e.g., money, property, a service), an agreement lacks sufficient consideration.

Contractual capacity: Both parties must possess the full legal capacity to assume contractual duties. Limitations to full capacity include mental illness and such diminished states as intoxication.

Lawful object: The purpose of the contract must be legal. A contract to commit an unlawful act or to violate public policy is void (without legal force).

Installation and Comissioning

Installation

Installation is the process of making hardware and/or software ready for use. Obviously, different systems require different types of installations. While certain installations are simple and straightforward and can be performed by non- professionals, others are more complex and time-consuming and may require the involvement of specialists.

Installation can be categorized into two broad categories: physical and virtual. Physical installation pertains to installing physical equipment such as computer hard drives, cables, modems and so on, while virtual installation refers to installation of software. Much physical machine installation requires specific expertise. Similarly, there are software installations that can be done only by experts, whereas other installations are as simple and straightforward as the wizard- based installations commonly found with consumer software and frequently available on websites to be downloaded. Different types of software installations include Windows Installer installation, web-based software installation and single exe software installation.

Comissioning

Commissioning means to run that same machine or device that was installed. to convert that dead machine into working condition properly according to the desired parameters on safe condition is known as commissioning.

Commissioning also includes things like checking oil levels, fluid levels, temperatures, pressures and for general issues that are contradictory to the intended correct operation of the equipment

What is the difference between 'installation' and 'commissioning'?

This has got to be one of the most frequently asked questions we tend to receive. A quick note to explain and clarify any confusion on the matter:

- To install an eligible installation means to build and/or put in place the relevant plant.
- To 'commission' a plant means to carry out all necessary tests and procedures required by industry standards to show that the plant is able to deliver heat for the purpose for which it was installed.

For smaller scale installations, installation and commissioning may happen on the same day.

However, for those dealing with the larger scale, there is usually a significant testing period, so the date of installation and date of commissioning may be different.

Feedback invoice

Use this free basic invoice template to simplify your billing process for any service rendered. This all-inclusive template allows you to enter client bill-to and ship-to information, the date, and invoice number details, as well as descriptions and totals for each invoiced item. The template automatically subtotals line-by-line item totals, and you can easily add in any discount, tax, shipping and handling, or other details that might affect the total for which you're billing.

Auto Repair Invoice

Use this automotive repair-specific invoice to detail the costs of parts and labor. This easy-to-fill invoice allows you to specify the client name, order number, relevant service dates, and mechanical details. It also provides space for you to include the following vehicle-specific information:

- Vehicle identification number (VIN)
- Odometer reading
- Make and model
- License number and state
- Motor number

Additionally, you can calculate labor and parts-specific amounts, the total-with-tax-rate percentage, and any other relevant variables.

Independent Contractor Invoice

This easy-to-use template is your perfect business partner, ensuring timely payment for services rendered as an independent contractor. Use this form to enter billable hours in meticulous detail, including a generous section for descriptions of work you have performed, start and end dates, hours, and your rate, which auto-calculates at the end of each row. Additionally, the template auto-calculates hours and monetary totals, giving you the ability to enter tax rates, miscellaneous costs, the grand total, and the actual total due. Show your clients your level of professionalism — and make sure you receive prompt payment for your services — with this reusable template, available in PDF and Excel formats.

Sales Invoice Template

Keep your business humming along with this easy-to-fill sales invoice template. Sales-specific fields allow you to enter the item number, quantity, unit price, subtotal, discount, tax, shipping and handling, and grand total. Save time by generating sales invoices with this reusable, fillable, and printable PDF and Excel template that you can easily save or send to invoice clients.

Rental Invoice

Make sure tenants pay their rent due in a timely fashion — and keep the property aspect of your books up to date — with this free, downloadable rental invoice template. It serves as a printable or electronic version of a rent invoice, and can also double as a past-due invoice to notify tenants of overdue rent. Customize tenant-specific details and ensure timely payment with the following sections: property address, rent, fees, total, and terms and conditions. This reusable template is available in Word and PDF formats.

Photography Invoice

Speed time invoicing and more time on what you do best: taking great photographs. Use this photography-specific, professional invoice to capture your time and effort, including photographer and company details as well as client contact information. This invoice template also includes a generous terms and remarks section, in which you can document and customize details and itemization for photoshoots, printing and production, row-by-row services, and individual photographic services.

Service Invoice

This reusable template serves as an invoice for any service that requires you to itemize your own (or your organization's) name, bill-to and ship-to information, description of services rendered, hours, rate, subtotals, tax, and final totals. This invoice template is simple to use and provides you with fields for unique invoice numbers, invoice dates, customer IDs, and any special terms related to the services you provide.

Pro Forma Invoice

With this unique template, create planned, or pro forma, invoices to capture the details of impending shipments of goods. For your goods, enter the shipment information, customs info, item number, unit of measure, description, quantity, unit value, freight, insurance, and total value. This invoice can serve as an agreed-upon contract for a transaction or as a confirmed purchase order for a shipment. The template is unique and includes an optional (and potentially legally binding) certification of an invoice's actual goods (i.e. how the exporter describes the goods in the invoice).

Graphic Design Invoice

Created specifically with design components in mind, this easy-to-fill graphic design invoice allows you to enter your contact information, client information, project name, and description of work. Customize your invoice with a terms and remarks section, and enter unique tests for clients to contact you with any questions concerning an invoice.

This reusable template is available in PDF and Word formats as an individual graphic design invoice template. Once you have entered the relevant information you want to appear on successive invoices, you can save the template as your standard invoice.

As a freelancer, you need a reliable way to bill your clients in order to ensure that they pay you correctly for the work you've done. Use this free, fillable, saveable, sendable, and freelance-specific PDF invoice template to fill in all relevant details, so you can invoice your clients and get on to the next gig. The template auto-calculates each line item of work, including the tax rate. Moreover, with generous space for the description of work, the hours worked, and your rate, this invoice template is perfect for keeping job-specific records and getting paid on time.

HVAC Invoice

Use this heating, ventilation, and air conditioning (HVAC) template to standardize your invoicing practice, so you can focus on delivering quality service to your clients. Avoid the unnecessary work of one-off invoicing or using templates or services that don't apply to your HVAC specialty with this easy-to-use, HVAC-specific PDF template that takes the guesswork out of invoicing.

Commercial Invoice

With this comprehensive commercial invoice template, reduce any delays or red tape by providing customs officers with a full description and history of goods. Use this template to document import, valuation, classification, and possible duty costs that international customs agents may levy. This all-inclusive commercial invoice template also offers space for the following details:

- Country and purpose of export
- Country of ultimate destination
- An international air waybill number
- Shipper export reference
- Consignee
- Full description of goods
- Harmonized System (HS) code
- Freight, insurance, and total costs

Trade Documents

Global flows of goods are not possible without a global flow of information. This must be exchanged between various stakeholders, including government authorities and transport intermediaries. The information is provided and exchanged in paper or electronic form, the so-called trade documents.

These trade documents and the data elements they contained are defined and prescribed by national and international regulatory requirements in fields such as health, consumer protection, safety, tax and revenue, trade policy, environment and security.

Examples of trade documents

Trade documents can be classified according to the sector in which they originated. The UNECE guidelines to Recommendation No.1 classify them into documents from commercial transaction sectors, payment sectors. transport and related services, and official control sectors.

Commercial transaction sector documents

These include documents exchanged between partners in international trade for information to tender, exchange between offerer and offeree, and the conclusion of a contract. Examples of such documents are offers and quotations, orders, Pro-forma invoices, and despatch advice.

Payment sector documents

These include documents exchanged between partners in international trade and their banks, as well as between banks for payments related to commercial transactions. They include, for example, commercial invoices, collection payment advice, documentary credit applications, and applications of bankers' draft and bankers' guarantees.

Transport and related service sector documents

These are documentary requirements of the procedures incidental to transport and related to the interface between trading partners and carriers; i.e. those related to forwarding and handling, and insuring. They include documents such as transport contracts (bills of lading, consignment notes), cargo freight manifests, freight invoices, arrival notices, insurance policies and warehouse receipts.

Official control documents

These are required for the control of goods conducted by various official bodies for the export, transit and import of goods. They include goods declaration for Customs purposes, SPS certificates, control and inspection certificates, and dangerous goods declarations.

Functions of trade documents

As shown above, trade documents have different origins, but they also serve different functions. They can act as contractual documents, such as insurance policies, bills of lading and commercial invoices. At the same time they support information during a different formality.

Paper documents (or electronic files) used in international trade that prove that certain events have taken place.All these documents are issued by exporters, shipping lines, airlines, international trucking companies, freight forwarders, logistics companies, customs, banks and insurance companies. Models of International Trade Documents.

CHAPTER IX

Industrial Legislation

Introduction

Factories Act, 1948 (India)

The Factories Act, 1948 (Act No. 63 of 1948), as amended by the Factories (Amendment) Act, 1987 (Act 20 of 1987), served to assist in formulating national policies in India with respect to occupational safety and health in factories and docks in India. It dealt with various problems concerning the safety, health, efficiency, and well-being of the persons at workplaces. It was replaced by the Occupational Safety, Health, and Working Conditions Code, 2020.

Factories Act, 1948

Emblem of India.SVG: Parliament of India

Enacted by: Parliament of India

Repealed by: Occupational Safety, Health, and Working Conditions Code, 2020

Status: Repealed

The Act is administered by the Ministry of Labour and Employment in India through its Directorate General Factory Advice Service & Labour Institutes (DGFASLI) and by the State Governments through their factory inspectorates. DGFASLI advises the Central and State Governments on the administration of the Factories Act and coordinating the factory inspection services in the States.

The Act is applicable to any factory using power & employing 10 or more workers and if not using power, employing 20 or more workers on any day of the preceding twelve months, and in any part of which a manufacturing process is being carried on with the aid of power, or is ordinarily so carried on, or whereon twenty or more workers are working or were working on any day of the preceding twelve months, and in any part of which a manufacturing process is being carried on without the aid of power, or is ordinarily so carried on; but this does not include a mine, or a mobile unit belonging to the armed forces of the union, a railway running shed or a hotel, restaurant or eating place.

The objective of the Factories Act,1948

The main objectives of the Indian Factories Act, 1948are to regulate the working conditions in factories, to regulate health, safety welfare, and annual leave, and enact special provisions in respect of young persons, women, and children who work in the factories.

1. Working Hours:

According to the provision of working hours of adults, no adult worker shall be required or allowed to work in a factory for more than 48 hours in a week. There should be a weekly holiday.

2. Health:

For protecting the health of workers, the Act lays down that every factory shall be kept clean and all necessary precautions shall be taken in this regard. The factories should have a proper drainage system, adequate lighting, ventilation, temperature, etc.

Adequate arrangements for drinking water should be made. Sufficient latrines and urinals should be provided at convenient places. These should be easily accessible to workers and must be kept clean.

3. Safety:

In order to provide safety to the workers, the Act provides that the machinery should be fenced, no young person shall work at any dangerous machine, in confined spaces, there should be provision for manÂholes of adequate size so that in case of emergency the workers can escape.

4. Welfare:

For the welfare of the workers, the Act provides that in every factory adequate and suitable facilities for washing should be provided and maintained for the use of workers.

Facilities for storing and drying clothing, facilities for sitting, first-aid appliances, shelters, rest roomsâ€™ and lunchrooms, crÃ¨ches, should be there.

5. Penalties:

The provisions of The Factories Act, 1948, or any rules made under the Act, or any order given in writing under the Act is violated, it is treated as an offence. The following penalties can be imposed:-

(a) Imprisonment for a term which may extend to one year;

(b) Fine which may extend to one lakh rupees; or

© Both fine and imprisonment.

If a worker misuses an appliance related to welfare, safety and health of workers, or in relation to discharge of his duties, he can be imposed a penalty of Rs. 500/-.

Employee State Insurance (ESI)

ESI stands for Employee State Insurance managed by the Employee State Insurance Corporation which is an autonomous body created by the law under the Ministry of Labour and Employment, Government of India.

This scheme was started for Indian workers. The workers are provided with a huge variety of medical, monetary and other benefits from the employer. Any non-seasonal factory and company having more than 10 employees (in some states it is 20 employees) who have a maximum salary of Rs. 21,000/- has to mandatorily register itself with the ESIC.

Under this scheme, the employer needs to contribute an amount of 3.25% of the total monthly salary payable to the employee whereas the employer needs to contribute only 0.75% of his monthly salary every month of the year. The only exemption to the employee in paying his contribution is whose salary is less than Rs. 176/- per day.

General Provident Fund (GPF)

What is the Full form of GPF?

The full form of GPF is General Provident Fund. GPF is a provident fund scheme that refers to government employees. In this system, government officials contribute some amount of their salaries to the account. The accrued balance is paid to the employee at the time of retirement or superannuation.

Eligibility criteria of GPF

The government worker must be an Indian citizen.

This account is mandatory for government workers in that certain salary level.

Private company workers are not qualified for this scheme.

How does GPF Operate

It serves as a tool for government employees to save money. To the GPF account, the employee is expected to contribute some portion of their salary annually over a set of time. The balance accrued in the employee's GPF account shall be returned to the employee by the time of the superannuation or retirement.

The holder of the GPF account must also nominate a nominee for their consideration. If something occurs to the account holder, the nominee will receive all the benefits.

The account also possesses a feature known as GPF advance. It is a type of interest-free loan from the GPF.

Bonus

A bonus payment is usually made to employees in addition to their base salary as part of their wages or salary. While the base salary usually is a fixed amount per month, bonus payments more often than not vary depending on known criteria, such as the annual turnover, or the net number of additional customers acquired, or the current value of the stock of a public company. Thus bonus payments can act as incentives for managers attracting their attention and their personal interest towards what is seen as gainful for their companies‘ economic success.

1. Gain or Profit Sharing

It is one of the most common and effective ways to give bonuses to your workforce. Here, employers dedicate a percentage of the profit for a certain period to the workers. This is very effective as it motivates the workforce to do better because the more the gain, the more is the bonus amount.

2. Spot Bonus

A spot bonus is a generous gift given to workers on the spot for completing a specific task. These are mostly cash prizes that can typically start from $50 and onwards. This bonus sparks the initiative characteristics of workers to perform above and beyond.

3. Non-Cash Bonus

Non-cash bonus is a cost-effective way to give a gesture of employee appreciation. These are generally a certificate, token of appreciation, or a trophy. You can reward these at the annual function along the lines of an award night for corporate excellence, etc.

4. Task Bonus

Task-based bonuses are employee rewards combined with specific tasks. Employees are entitled to get a prize when they finish the task allotted to the bonus. This bonus is an excellent incentive mechanism to enhance job efficiency and effectiveness.

5. Sign-On

A sign-on bonus is a reward you give to new hires in their onboarding process. While this bonus was meant for athletes, different companies nowadays offer similar bonuses to their new joiners. It makes the new hires feel valued and paints a great image of the employer.

6. Holiday Bonus

This may be the most common bonus that most employers give to their workers. A holiday bonus is a gift to workers during the different festivals of the year. This practice of holiday bonus is mainly prevalent during Thanksgiving, Christmas, and New Year periods.

7. Gift Cards

Gift Cards are some of the most common forms of non-cash-based bonuses you can give to your workers. Millennials increasingly use these to get a great deal on their favorite products. It is also a cost-effective type of reward for employers since most gift cards don't cost much.

8. Referral Bonus

Referral Bonus is a great alternative to include in your rewards and recognition program and to help with your HR department's workload management. Referral Bonus is given when an existing worker recommends an acquaintance of his/her for a job.

Trade Unions

Labour unions or trade unions are organizations formed by workers from related fields that work for the common interest of its members. They help workers in issues like the fairness of pay, good working environment, hours of work, and benefits. They represent a cluster of workers and provide a link between the management and workers.

Trade Unions are voluntary organizations of Workers as well as Employers formed to protect and promote the interest of their members. They are the most suitable organizations for balancing and improving the relations between the employer and the employees. Trade Unions have made headway due to rapid industrial development. The workers come together to maintain and improve their bargaining power on wages and working conditions. The first organized Trade Union in India named the Madras Labour Union was formed in the year 1918. From the beginning itself, Trade Unions were not confined to workers alone. From the 19th Century itself, there were Employer's associations in the form of Chamber of Commerce, Industrial Associations, etc. to protect and promote the interests of their members in a concerted manner. After independence, expansion of industrial activity and growing worker's Trade Unions acted as a spur for strengthening and expansion of employers' organization.

Description: The purpose of these unions is to look into the grievances of wagers and present a collective voice in front of the management. Hence, it acts as the medium of communication between the workers and management.

Regulation of relations, settlement of grievances, raising new demands on behalf of workers, collective bargaining and negotiations are the other key principle functions that these trade unions perform.

The Trade Unions Act 1926 has been amended from time to time, the most important being the Trade Unions (Amendment) Act, 2001. This Act has been enacted in order to bring more transparency and to provide greater support to trade unionism in India. Some of the salient features of the Trade Unions (Amendment) Act, 2001 are:

- No trade union of workmen shall be registered unless at least 10% or 100, whichever is less, subject to a minimum of 7 workmen engaged or employed in the establishment or industry with which it is connected, are the members of such trade union on the date of making of an application for registration
- A registered trade union of workmen shall at all times continue to have not less than 10% or 100 of the workmen, whichever is less, subject to a minimum of 7 persons engaged or employed in the establishment or industry with which it is connected, as its members.
- A provision for filing an appeal before the Industrial Tribunal / Labour Court in case of non-registration or for restoration of registration has been provided.
- All office bearers of a registered trade union, except not more than one-third of the total number of office bearers or five, whichever is less, shall be persons actually engaged or employed in the establishment or industry with which the trade union is connected.
- Minimum rate of subscription by members of the trade union is fixed at Rs 1 per annum for rural workers, three rupees per annum for workers in other unorganized sectors and Rs 12 rupees per annum in all other cases.
- The employees who have been retired or have been retrenched shall not be construed as outsiders for the purpose of holding an office in the trade union concerned
- For the promotion of civic and political interest of its members, unions are authorized to set up separate political funds.

The Indian Trade Union Act, 1926, is the principle act which controls and regulates the mechanism of trade unions. In India, political lines and ideologies influence trade union movements. This is the reason why today political parties are forming and running trade unions

In India the Trade Union movement is generally divided into political lines. According to provisional statistics from the Ministry of Labour, trade unions had a combined membership of 24,601,589 in 2002. As of 2008, there are 11 Central Trade Union Organisations (CTUO) recognised by the Ministry of Labour.

Central Trade Unions:

1. All India Trade Union Congress (AITUC)
2. Bharatiya Mazdoor Sangh (BMS)
3. Centre of Indian Trade Unions (CITU)
4. Hind Mazdoor Kisan Panchayat (HMKP)
5. Hind Mazdoor Sabha (HMS)
6. Indian Federation of Free Trade Unions (IFFTU)
7. Indian National Trade Union Congress (INTUC)
8. National Front of Indian Trade Unions (NFITU)
9. National Labor Organization (NLO)
10. Trade Unions Co-ordination Centre (TUCC)
11. United Trade Union Congress (UTUC) and
12. United Trade Union Congress - Lenin Sarani (UTUC- LS)

Industrial Disputes

To understand the scope of the Industrial Disputes Act, 1947 it is important to understand the meaning and import of the terms 'industrial dispute' and 'industry' as defined in the statute. Section 2(k) of the Act states that the former describes any dispute or difference between employers and employees, or between employers and workmen, or amongst workmen, which is connected with the employment or non-employment or the terms of employment or with the conditions of employment of any person. Section 2(j) of the Act defines the latter as any business, trade, undertaking, manufacture, or calling of employers and includes any calling, service, employment, handicraft, or industrial occupation or avocation of workmen.

Therefore, to attract the application of the Act, a dispute would have to occur in an establishment falling under the definition of industry and would have to involve one or more of the stakeholders mentioned in the definition of industrial disputes. In other cases, there is no scope for governmental interference and thus the only recourse is to approach courts or engage in alternate dispute resolution mechanisms.

It is pertinent to note that the definition of 'industry' has been discussed extensively in case laws. In the landmark case of Bangalore Water Supply and Sewerage Board v. R. Rajappa, the Supreme Court laid down a three-pronged test to ascertain whether a particular activity was industrial in nature. If the said activity involved systematic and organized activity, cooperation between employer and employee, and was carried out for the production of goods and services, it would be considered industrial in nature. The elements of capital investment and profit motive were held to be immaterial in the determination of the above question. In the case of an undertaking engaging in multiple activities, which might or might not be one of the core activities, the Dominant Nature Test is applicable. It determines whether a specific activity of any enterprise can be classified as industrial in nature by examining the predominant nature of the activities conducted by the enterprise and the integrated nature of the departments.

Causes of Industrial Disputes

The causes of industrial disputes can be broadly classified into two categories:

- **Economic Causes**

The economic causes will include issues relating to compensation like wages, bonuses, allowances, and conditions for work, working hours, leave and holidays without pay, unjust layoffs, and retrenchments.

- **Non-Economic Causes**

The non-economic factors will include victimization of workers, ill-treatment by staff members, sympathetic strikes, political factors, indiscipline, etc.

Industrial dispute means any dispute of difference between employees and employers or between employers and workmen or between workmen and workmen, which is connected with the employment or non-employment of the terms of employment or the conditions of work of any person (The industrial Disputes Act 1947, Section 2K).

Every human being (say a labour) has certain requirements/needs e.g., economic needs, social needs, security requirements. When these requirements do not get satisfied, there arises a conflict between the worker and the capitalist/employer.

Industrial disputes are of two types i.e., individual disputes and collective disputes. The individual disputes may be disputes such as reinstatement, compensation for wrong termination etc. Disputes relating to wages, bonus, profit-sharing hours of work etc. are collective disputes.

Industrial Disputes Act, 1947

The Industrial Disputes Act, 1947 extended to the whole of India and regulated Indian labour law so far as that concerns trade unions as well as Individual workmen employed in any Industry within the territory of Indian mainland. Enacted on 11 March 1947 and It came into force 1 April 1947. It was replaced by the Industrial Relations Code, 2020.

Whole the history of labour struggle indicates the continuous demand for a fair return to labour. INDUSTRIAL DISPUTE are mainly the result of dissatisfaction amongst the labour as regards their existing labour conditions. With the above in mind, the INDUSTRIAL dispute act came into force in 1947 and aims at settling the industrial disputes on a new patter known under the act as adjudication.

Authorities Under This Act For Settlement Of Industrial Dispute Works Committee

Any industry, in which 100 or more workers are and have been employed on any day in the preceding 12 months, shall constitute a works committee.

Works committee shall have representatives of both workers and employers both. Workmen representatives will not be less than those of employers in number.

Works committee shall promote measures for securing and improving amity and good relations between the worker and employer. It will comment upon matters of their common interest and try to compose any material difference of opinion in respect of such matters.

Works committee shall smooth away friction that might arise between the workers and the employer in day-to-day work.

Minimum Wage

minimum wage is the lowest salary or payment that employers have to get legally from their workers. Moreover, it is the price bar below which workers may not sell their labour. Though there are several laws in support of this in every jurisdiction not all organisations practice it lawfully

The idea of bringing is believed to increase the standard of living of workers and reduce inequality and poverty. But people who oppose this say that giving minimum wages will only increase unemployment and poverty. They also believe that this harms the businesses because high minimum wages will expect businesses to raise the prices of their product or service to accommodate the extra expense of paying a higher wage.

Minimum wage Act, 1948

The granting of minimum wages to the workers is one of the essential requirements. The wages should be sufficient to maintain the worker and his family. The object of the Act is to prevent the exploitation of workers. The minimum wages Act is a piece of social legislation intended to do social justice to the workers.

The Act extends to the whole of India. It came on 15th March 1948. It applies to the employment which is listed in the schedule of the Act and in certain cases be extended to any other employment by the government

The necessity of the Act

The workers are poorly organised and they cannot fight with the employer

Trade unions of workers are weak.

To fix the minimum wages and make it obligatory for the employer to pay to the workers.

By granting minimum wages, industrial peace is maintained.

To avoid malpractice by the employer in payment of wages to the workers.

Important Terms of the Act

Appropriate Government: This means either the central Government or the state government, depending upon the type of employment

Competent Authority: It means the authority appointed by the appropriate Government by notification to ascertain from time to time the cost of living index number applicable to the employees in the scheduled employment.

Cost of Living Index Number: It means the index number ascertained and declared by the competent authority by notification in the Official Gazette to be the cost of living index number.

Wages: It means all remuneration capable of being expressed in terms of money be payable to a person employed in respect of his employment. It includes basic wages, dearness, bonus, and house rent.

Minimum wages: It represents the level below which wage cannot be allowed to drop. It should provide not nearly for existence, but for maintaining the efficiency of the worker. Minimum wages should also provide for some measure of education, medical requirements, and other amenities. The minimum wages are fixed on the cost of living index.

Salient features of Minimum Wages Act

- Fixation of minimum wages
- Procedure for fixing and revising minimum wages
- Fixation of hours of work
- Method of payments
- Maintenance of registers and records
- Inspection
- Penalties

Fixation of Minimum Waves: The act provides the procedure for fixation of minimum wages for the following workers :

- Different scheduled employments
- Different classes of work in the same scheduled employment
- Adults, children, apprentice
- Different localities

Minimum rates of wages may be fixed by any one or more of the following wage periods:

- By the hour
- By the day
- By the month
- By such other larger wage period as may be prescribed.

The following considerations will be taken into account in the fixation of the minimum wages:

- The prevailing economic consideration.
- The cost of living place
- The nature of the work to be performed; and
- The conditions in which the work is be performed.

Procedure for fixing and Revising Minimum Wages :

Appointing the committees by the Government. Which will hold inquiries and give advice, in respect of fixation or revision of minimum wages.

By notification in the official gazette, publish its proposal for the information of the person likely to be affected thereby and specified date, not less than two months from the date of notification, of which the proposal will be taken into consideration.

On to the information and advice, the minimum wages are fixed or revised.

Fixation of Hours of work: Where minimum wages in respect of any scheduled employment have been fixed, the appropriate Govt. May:

- Fix the number of hours for a normal working day inclusive of one or more specified intervals.
- provide for a day of rest in every period of seven days.
- provide for payment of remuneration in respect of such days of rest.
- Overtime shall be paid at the rate fixed under the act. These are generally double the normal rates.

Methods of payments:

In a factory employing 1000 or fewer workers, the wages must be paid within seven days after the competition of the month.

In a factory employing more than 1000 workers, the wages must be paid within ten days after the completion of the month.

Maintenance of Registers and Records: The employer is required to keep proper records and Registers for payment of wages to each worker. The following details of each worker should be available:

- Rates of wages payable.
- The number of days in which overtime claimed by the worker.
- The deductions to be made from wages.
- The wages actually paid and date of payment.

All other relevant details.

Inspection: The appropriate Govt. appoint inspectors for the enforcement of the Act. The inspector van enters any premises and can inspect the documents of wages which he thinks fit for enforcing the rules, under the act.

Penalties: The act is administered by the state Govt. If an employer pays less than the minimum rate of wages or violates any other provisions of the act, he can be punished with imprisonment up to six months or with a fine up to Rs 500/-(five hundred) or both.

The main objective of the Minimum Wages Act 1948, is Fixing a Minimum Rate of Wages in a number of Industries where the Labors are Not Organized and Sweated Labors are most dominant.

There is strong evidence that the minimum wage boosts the earnings of the lowest wage workers, and it may boost the earnings of those earning moderately higher hourly wages. In almost every wage study, the effect is more marked for women, who are more likely than men to be in low-wage positions.

Compensation

Employee Compensation Definition:

Compensation is the total cash and non-cash payments that you give to an employee in exchange for the work they do for your business. It is typically one of the biggest expenses for businesses with employees. Compensation is more than an employee's regular paid wages. It also includes many other types of wages and benefits.

Types of compensation include:

- Base pay (hourly or salary wages)
- Sales commission
- Overtime wages
- Tip income
- Bonus pay
- Recognition or merit pay
- Benefits (insurances, standard vacation policy, retirement)
- Stock options
- Other non-cash benefits

What is base pay?

Base pay is the initial payment you give your employees. The base pay rate is essentially the minimum amount an employee can expect to receive before taxes and other deductions.

Base pay includes an employee's base salary or hourly wages. It also includes shift differentials and pays for special assignments.

Base salary vs. total compensation

An employee's base pay does not include compensation that might raise the wages above the base level. For example, bonuses, overtime, and commissions are not part of base pay. These types of pay are included in the employee's total compensation.

Apprenticeship

Before we dive into the scope of how apprenticeships can benefit organizations, let us understand the correct meaning of the term. Vocabulary.com defines "Apprenticeship as a kind of job training that involves following and studying a master of the trade on the job instead of in school. Carpenters, masons, doctors, and many other professionals often learn their trade through apprenticeship.

This is the universal definition to apprentice, and it is no different from the original and founding definition of Apprenticeship in India from The Apprentice Act, 1961. "Apprenticeship Training" means a course of training in any industry or establishment undergone in pursuance of a contract of apprenticeship and under prescribed terms and conditions which may be different for different categories of apprentices."

Apprenticeship training is one of the most efficient ways to develop a skilled workforce for any industry by using training facilities available in the establishments without the need to set up an independent training infrastructure. In line with the benefits that were identified for promoting apprenticeship in the country, comprehensive amendments to Apprentices Act 1961 are made periodically. The Act has been made more responsive to industry and youth. Employers can now engage up to 10% of their total workforce as apprentices. As a result, the number of apprentices in the country has increased from 2.70 lakh to 3.10 lakh in the past year.

While not even 30% of Indian companies hire apprentices, world nations operate on the apprentice-to-employee approach to employment. In a survey commissioned by the UK government in 2017, 86% of employers reported benefiting from 'the development of skills relevant to the organization' by hiring apprentices.

Payment of wages Act

With the growth of industries in India, problems relating to the payment of wages to persons employed in the industry took an ugly turn. The industrial units were riot making payment of wages to their workers at regular intervals and wages were not uniform. The industrial workers were forced to raise their heads against their exploitation. The Payment of Wages Bill, 1935 having been passed by the Legislative Assembly received its assent on 23rd April 1936. It came on the Statute Book as THE PAYMENT OF WAGES ACT, 1936 (4 of 1936).

The Payment of Wages Act, 1936 regulates the payment of wages to employees (direct and indirect). The act is intended to be a remedy against unauthorized deductions made by

The main objective for the introduction of the Payment of Wages Act, 1936, is to avoid unnecessary delay in the payment of wages and to prevent unauthorized deductions from the wages.

Applicability of Payment of Wages Act

As per section 1(6) of the Payment of Wages Act, the wages averaging less than INR 6,500 per month are covered and protected by the Act. Further, the Act is applicable to the payment of wages to persons employed in factories, upon railways, or in another establishment, as specified in the Payment of Wages Act.

Definition of Wages

The term wages has been defined as all remuneration (whether by way of salary, allowances, or otherwise) payable to a person employed in respect of his employment or of work done in such employment. Under the Payment of Wages Act, wages include:

Any remuneration payable under any award or settlement between the parties or order of a Court;

Any remuneration to which the person employed is entitled in respect of overtime work or holidays or any leave period;

Any additional remuneration payable under the terms of employment (whether called a bonus or by any other name);

Any sum which by reason of the termination of employment of the person employed is payable under any law, contract, or instrument which provides for the payment of such sum, whether with or without deductions, but does not provide for the time within which the payment is to be made;

Any sum to which the person employed is entitled under any scheme framed under any law for the time being in force, but does not include:

Any bonus (whether under a scheme of profit sharing or otherwise) which does not form part of the remuneration payable under the terms of employment or which is not payable under any award or settlement between the parties or order of a Court;

The value of any house accommodation, or of the supply of light, water, medical attendance or other amenity or of any service excluded from the computation of wages by a general or special order of the appropriate Government;

Any contribution paid by the employer to any pension or provident fund, and the interest which may have accrued thereon;

Any travelling allowance or the value of any travelling concession;

Any sum paid to the employed person to defray special expenses entailed on him by the nature of his employment; or

Any gratuity is payable on the termination of employment.

Due Date for Salary Payment and Wages

As per the provisions of the Payment of Wages Act, 1936, wages need to be paid to employees before the expiry of the 7th day of the last day of the wage period, where number of employees are less than 1000. In case the number of employee is less than 1000, wages must be paid before the expiry of the 10th day of the last day of the wage period.

Further, wages must be paid only on working days and not on holiday. In case the employment of any person is terminated, the wages earned by him must be paid before the expiry of the second working day from the date of termination.

Mode of Payment of Salary and Wages

Salary and wages should be paid only in current coins currency notes or both. The wages can also be paid by cheque or by credit into a bank account, however, in order to do so, the employer has to obtain written authorization from the employed person. Under the act, payment has to be made in currency notes or coins. Cheque payment or credit to the bank account is allowed with consent in writing by the employee. (Section 6).

Regular Pay

Payment should be made before the 7th day of a month where the number of workers is less than 1000 and 10th day otherwise. The wage period shall not exceed 1 month. The Act is applicable only to employees drawing wages not exceeding Rs. 6500 a month. [20]

Deduction from Wages

Employer is allowed to effect only authorized deductions, as specified in the Act. This includes fines (Section 8), absence from duty (Section 9), Damages or loss (Section 10), the deduction for services (amenities) given to employer (Section 11) recovery of advances and loans (Section 12, 13) and payment to cooperative society and insurance (Section 13).

The authority, on receipt of the application, will hear the applicant and the employer or other person responsible for the delay in payment of wages. On being satisfied, the authority may direct the employer to refund the excess deduction or may direct to make payment of wages together with the payment of compensation. The compensation amount cannot exceed 10 times the amount deducted and cannot exceed INR 3000, but the same should not be less than INR 1500.

Compensation is not payable in cases where authority is satisfied that:

The delay was due to bona fide error/dispute as to the amount payable to the employed person;

The person responsible was unable to make a payment due to exceptional circumstances, even though exercised due diligence;

The delay was due to the failure of the employed person to apply for or accept payment.

An appeal can be filed against the order of the authority, within 30 days before a court of small causes and/or before the district court.

Commercial Establishment Act

The shops and commercial establishments covered under the Act must mandatorily apply for registration under the respective state Act. All establishments and businesses, including the people working and maintaining a business from home, must obtain a Shop and Establishment Registration Certificate or Shop License ("Certificate") under the Act.

Commercial Establishment: Commercial Establishment means a commercial or trading or banking or insurance establishment, an establishment or administrative service in which persons employed are mainly engaged in office work, a hotel, restaurant, boarding or eating house, a café or any other refreshment house, a theatre or any other place of public amusement or entertainment.

The proprietors who run a business from home without having any physical store or premises are also required to obtain this Certificate. The proprietors of e-commerce business or online business, or online stores and establishments must register under this Act and obtain the Certificate. Every shop and commercial establishment should register itself under the Act within 30 days of commencement of business.

The Certificate or the Shop License acts as a basic registration/license for the business. This Certificate is produced for obtaining many other business licenses and registrations. It serves as proof of the incorporation of commercial establishments or shops. It is also useful when the proprietor of the business wants to obtain a loan or create a current bank account for the business. Most banks will ask for this Certificate for opening a current bank account.

Regulations under the Shop and Establishment Act

The Act, among other things, regulates the following matters-

- Hours of work, annual leave, weekly holidays.
- Payment of wages and compensation.
- Prohibition of employment of children.
- Prohibition of employing women and young persons in the night shift.
- Enforcement and Inspection.
- Interval for rest.
- Opening and closing hours.
- Record keeping by the employers.
- Dismissal provisions.

Process for Obtaining Shop and Establishment Registration

The procedure for obtaining the Shop and Establishment Registration Certificate differs from state to state. It can be obtained online or offline.

For obtaining the registration certificate online, the proprietor or owner of the shop or business must log into the respective State Labour Department website. The proprietor or owner must fill the application form for registration under the Shop and Establishment Act, upload the documents and pay the prescribed fees. The prescribed fees differ from state to state. Once the registration form is approved, the registration certificate will be issued online to the proprietor or owner of the business.

For obtaining the registration certificate offline, the registration application is to be filled and submitted to the Chief Inspector of the concerned area along with the prescribed fees. The Chief Inspector will issue the registration certificate to the owner or proprietor after being satisfied with the correctness of the application.

The registration application form contains the details relating to the name of the employer and establishment, address and category of the establishment, number of employees and other relevant details as required. The registration application needs to be renewed before the expiry of the period of registration. The validity of the Shop and Establishment Certificate differs from state to state. Some states provide the Certificate valid for a lifetime, while other states provide the Certificate valid for one to five years.

Exemptions from Registration:

Following organizations are exempted from registration.

- Offices of, or under the central or state government, or local authorities, except commercial undertaking.

- Any railway service, water transport service, postal, telegraph or telephone service, any system of public conservation or sanitation or any industry, or services like water, power, light to the public.
- Railway dining cars.
- Establishments for the treatment or care of the handicapped or mentally unfit.
- Establishments of the food corporation of India.
- Offices of legal practitioners and medical practitioners in which not more than 3 persons are employed.
- Offices of the bank.

Hence, to regulate conditions of work and employment in shops, commercial establishments, residential hotels, restaurants, eating houses, theatres, other places of public entertainment, and other establishments. Provisions include Regulation of Establishments, Employment of Children, Young Persons and Women, Leave and Payment of Wages, Health and Safety, etc.

www.ingramcontent.com/pod-product-compliance
Ingram Content Group UK Ltd.
Pitfield, Milton Keynes, MK11 3LW, UK
UKHW021907190726
13853UKWH00002B/555